Bold and Easy

Big Print Coloring Book

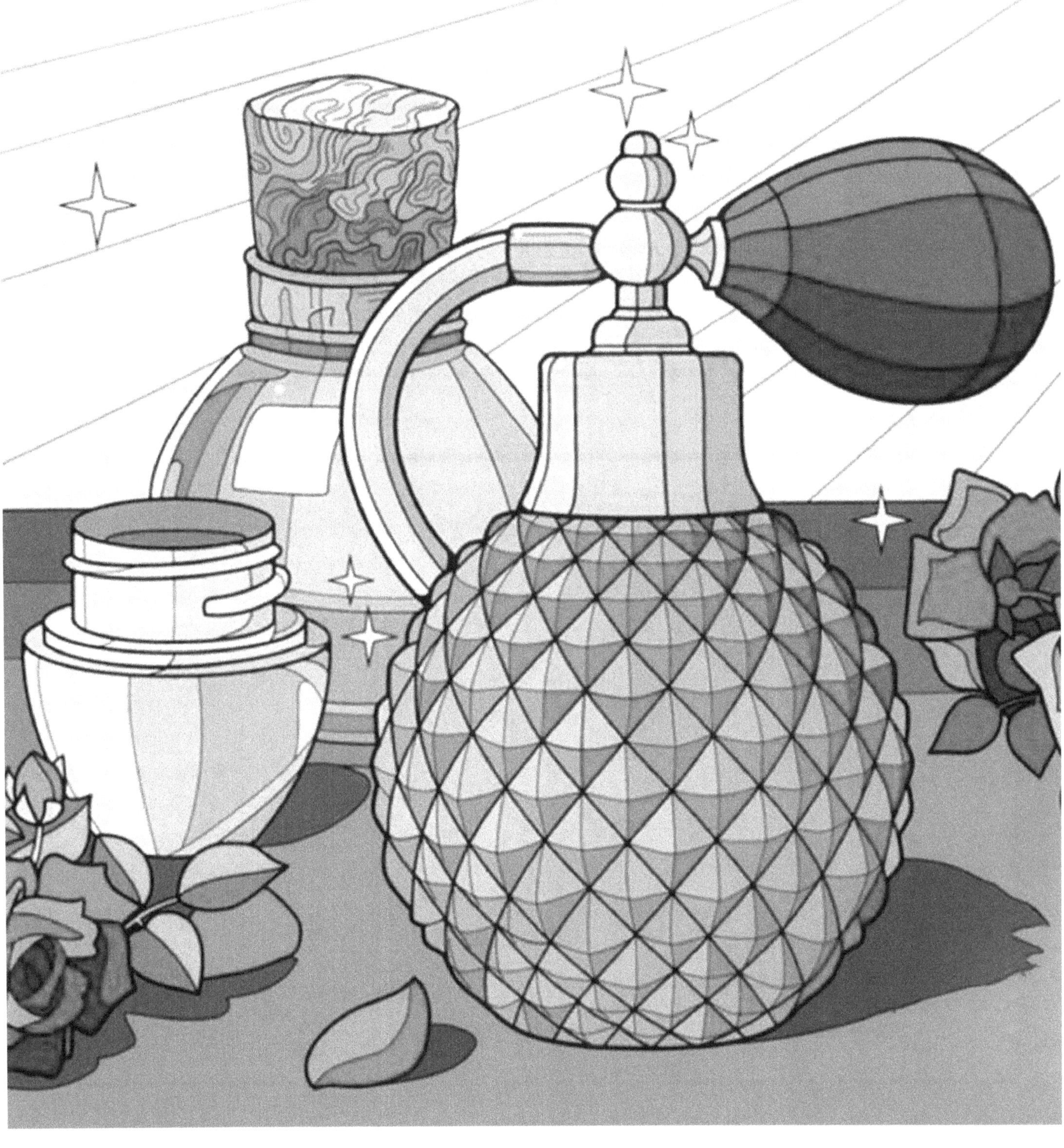

this book belongs to

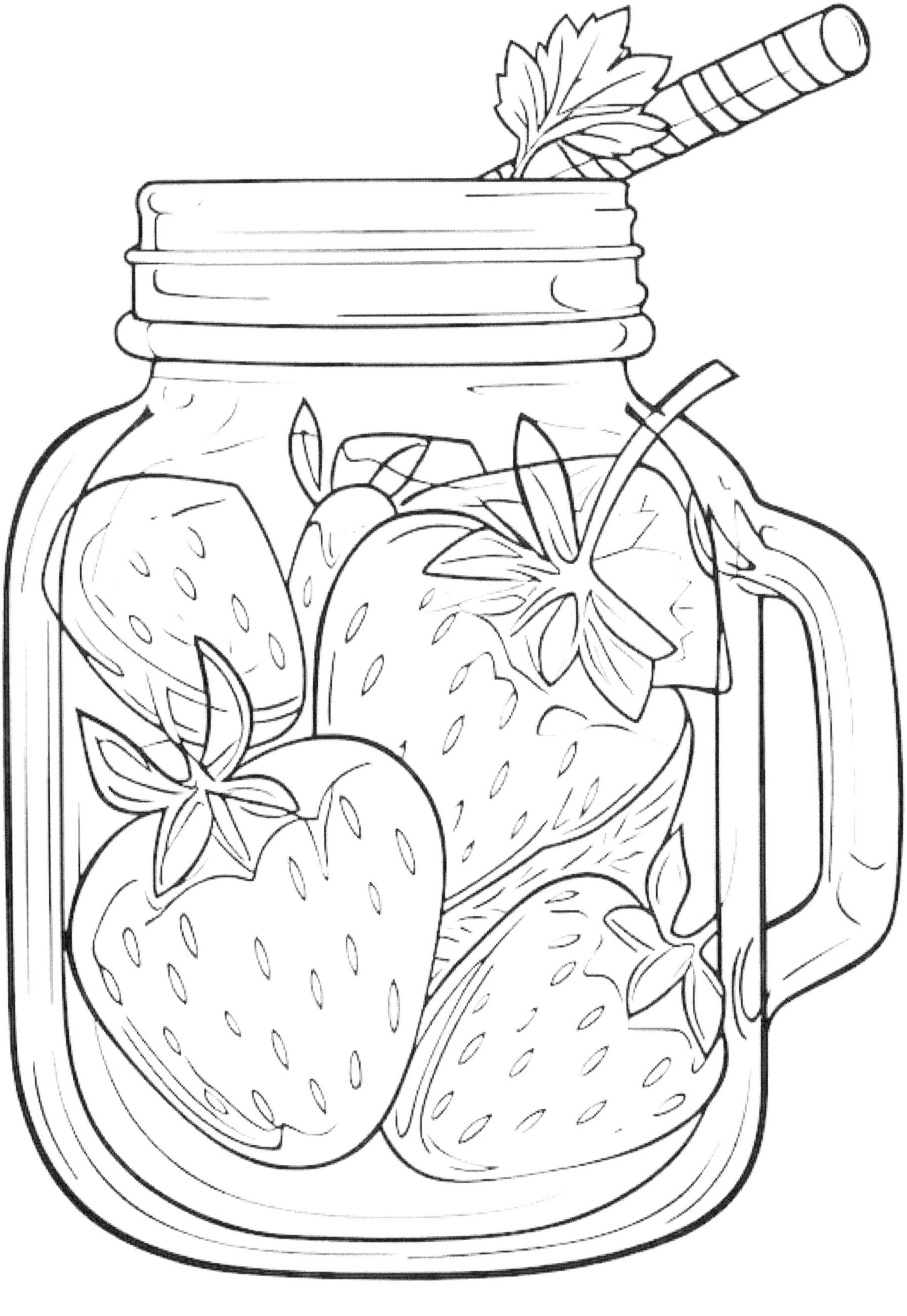

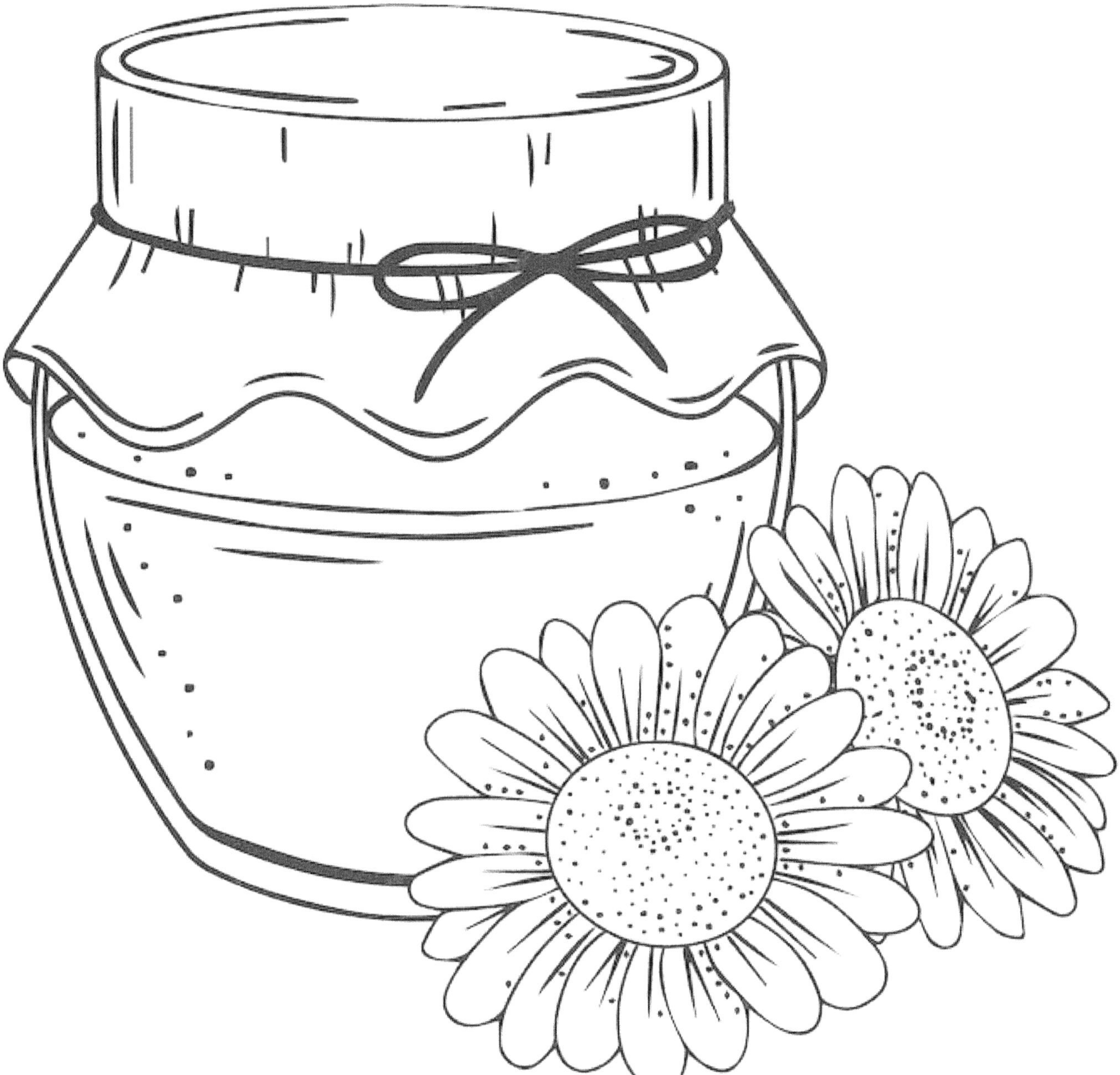

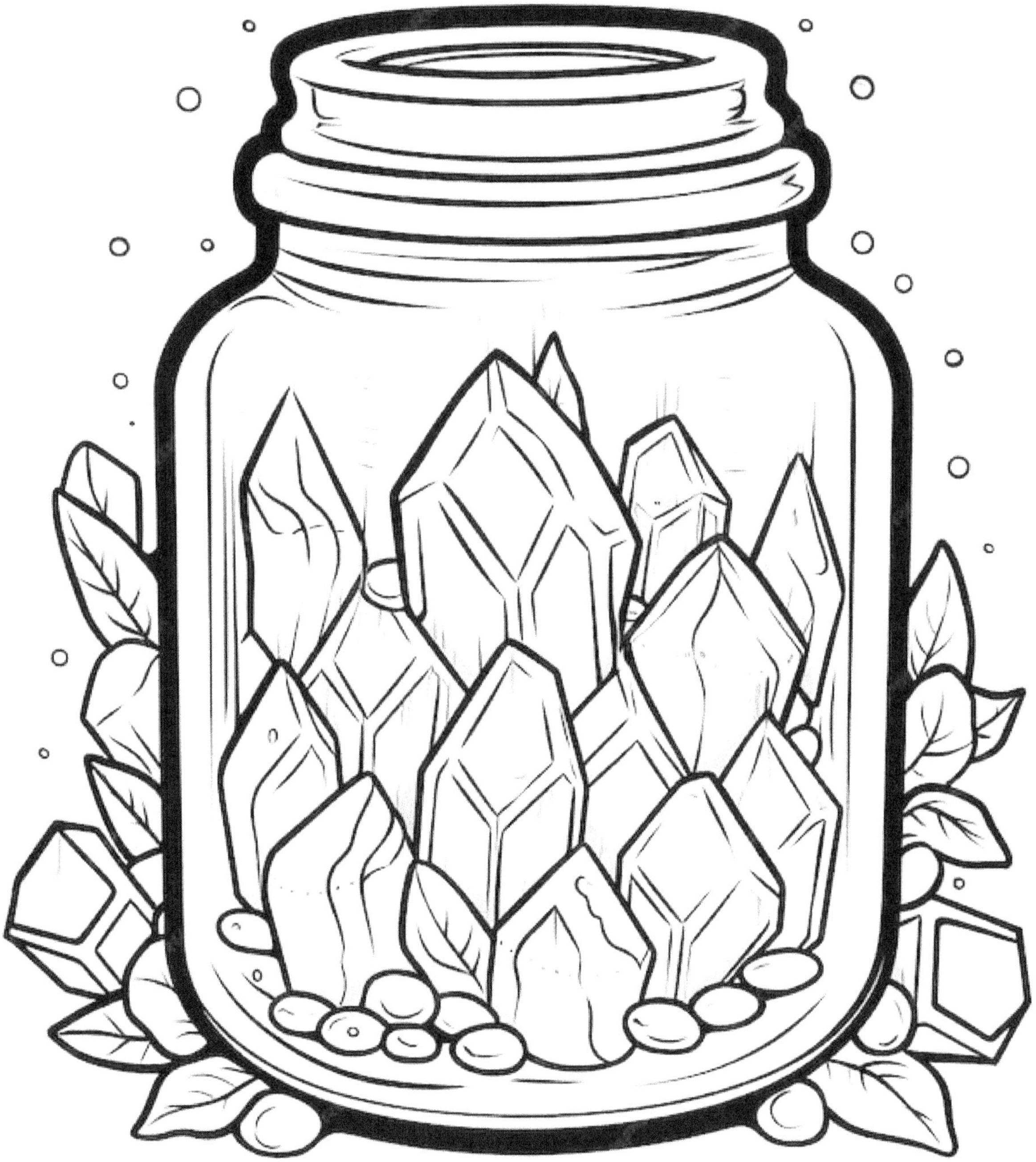

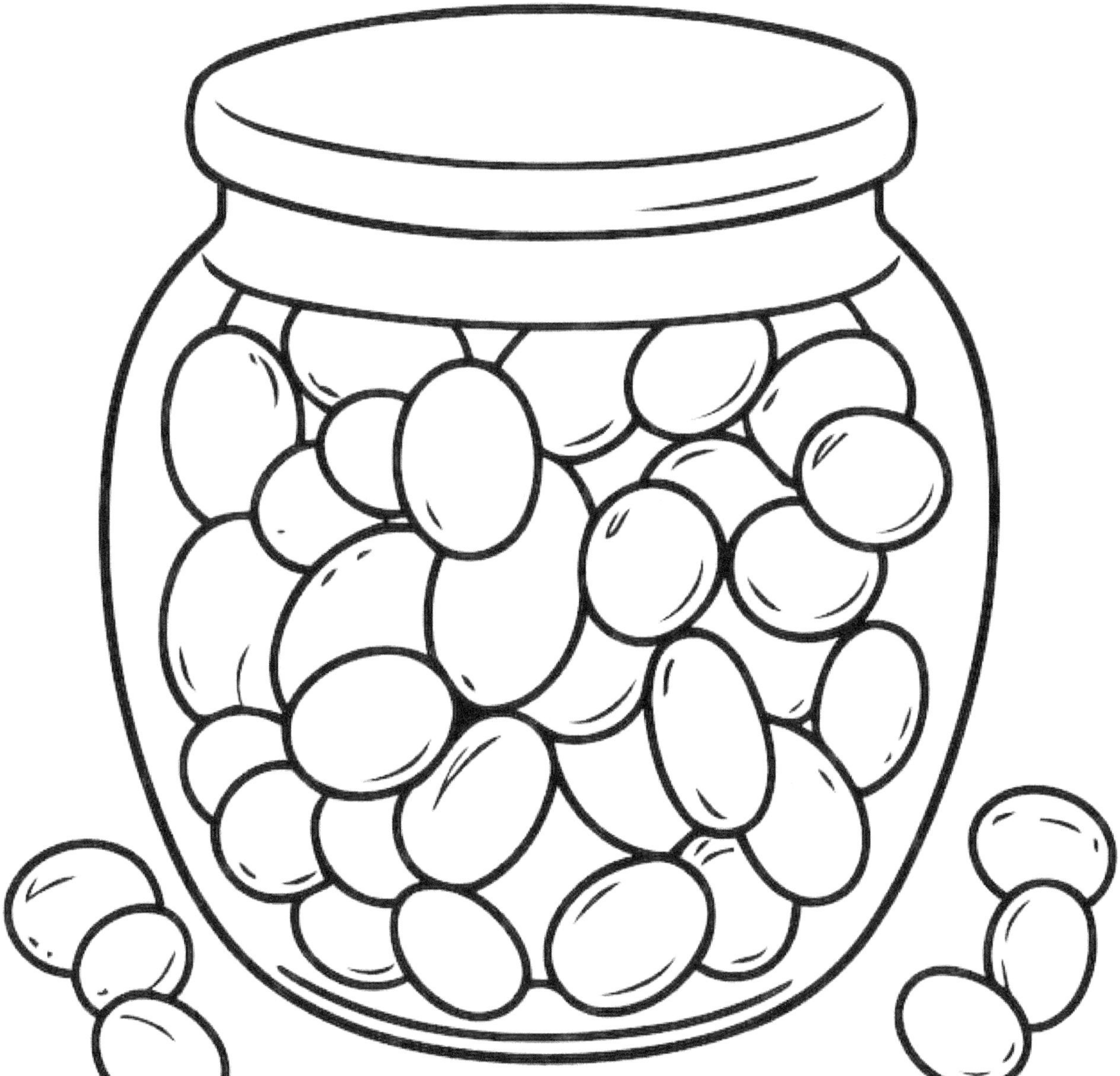

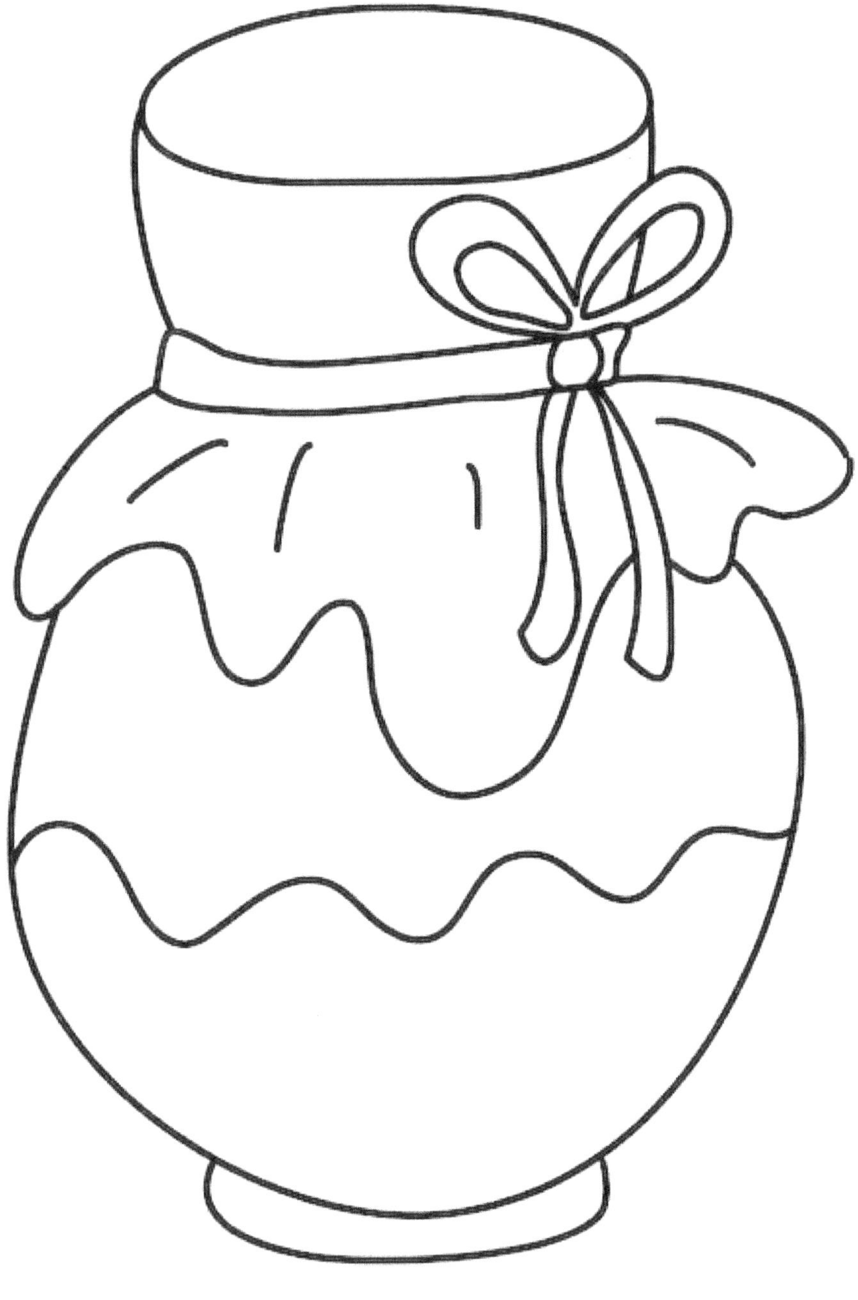

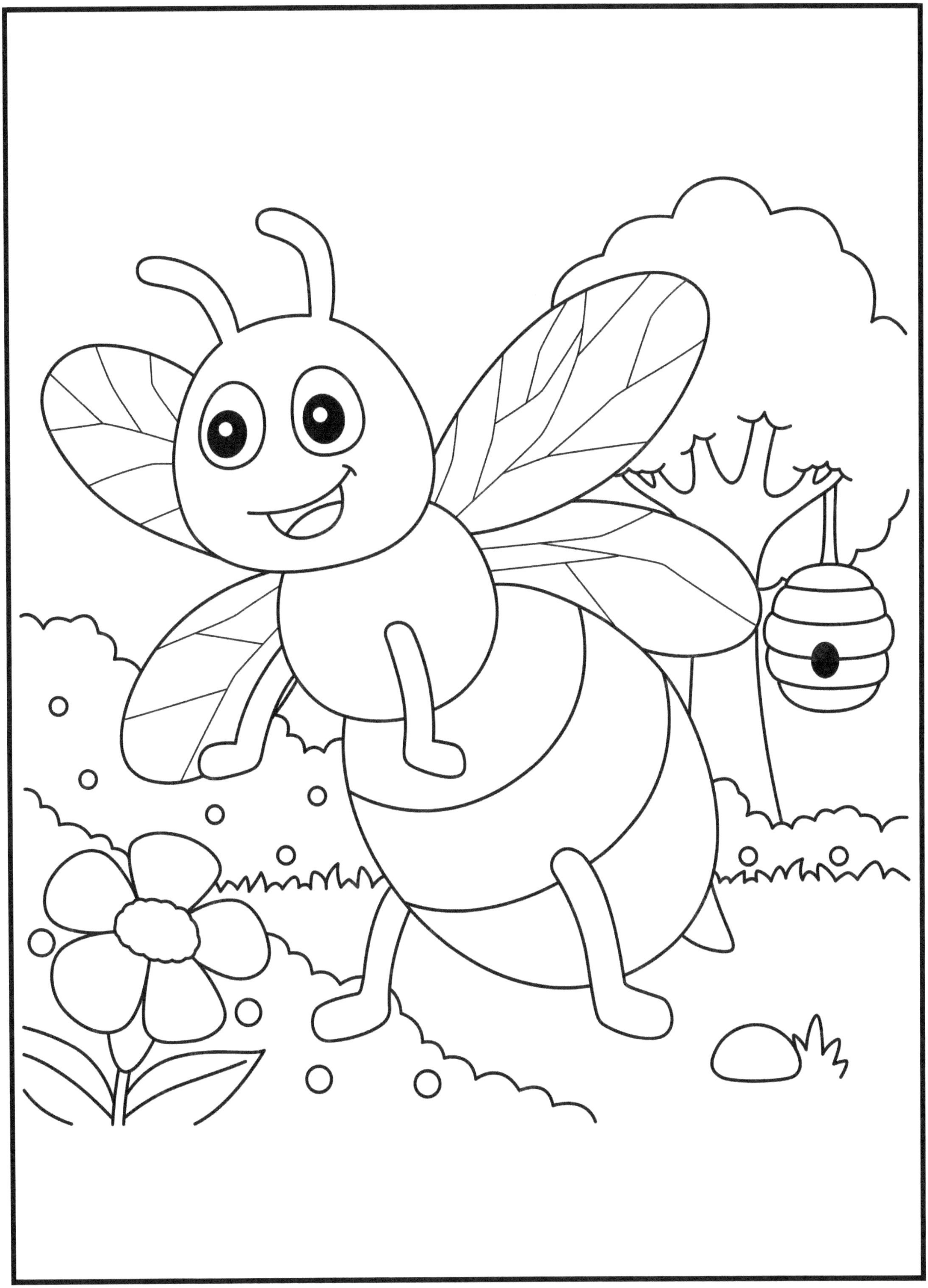

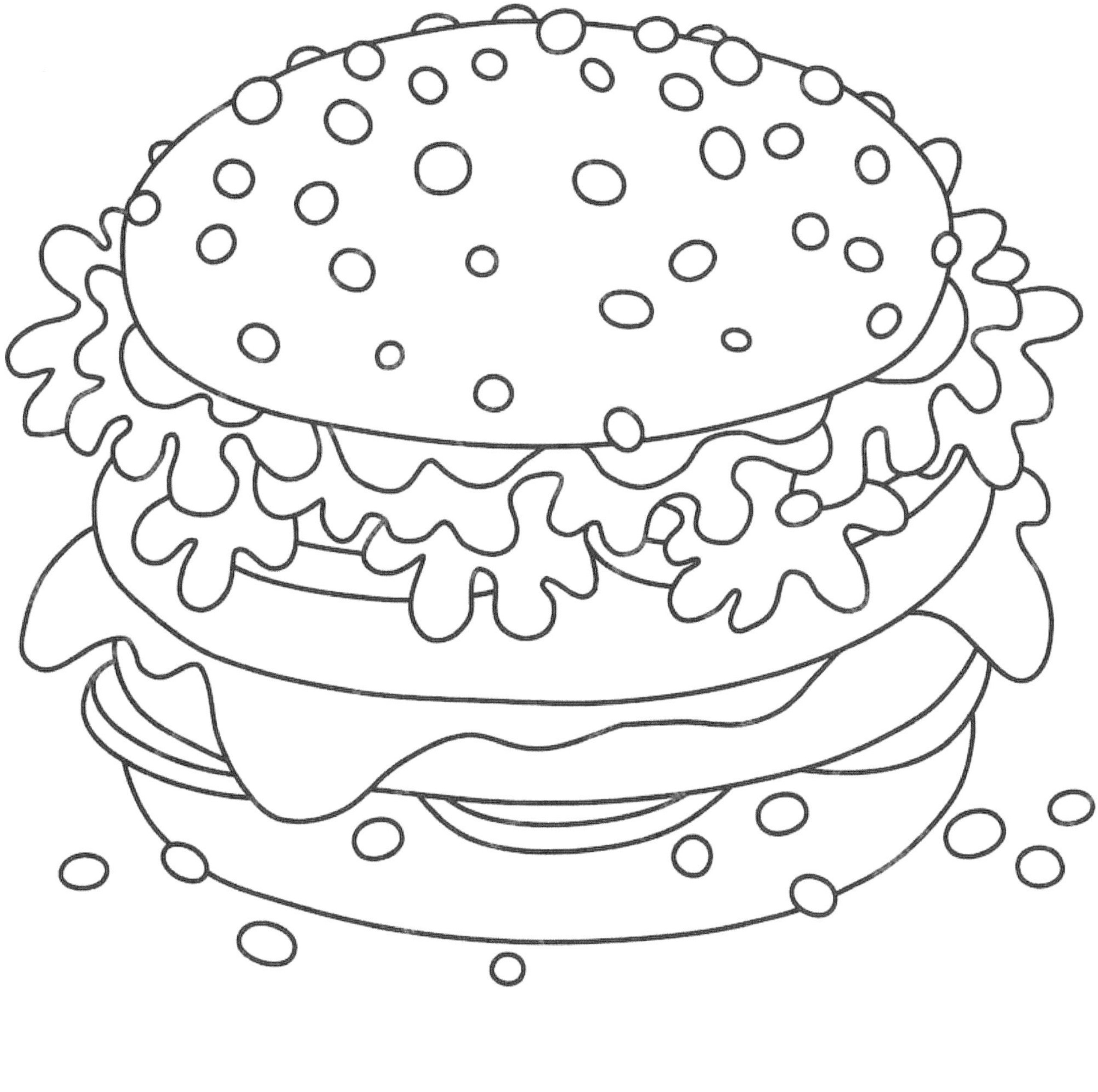

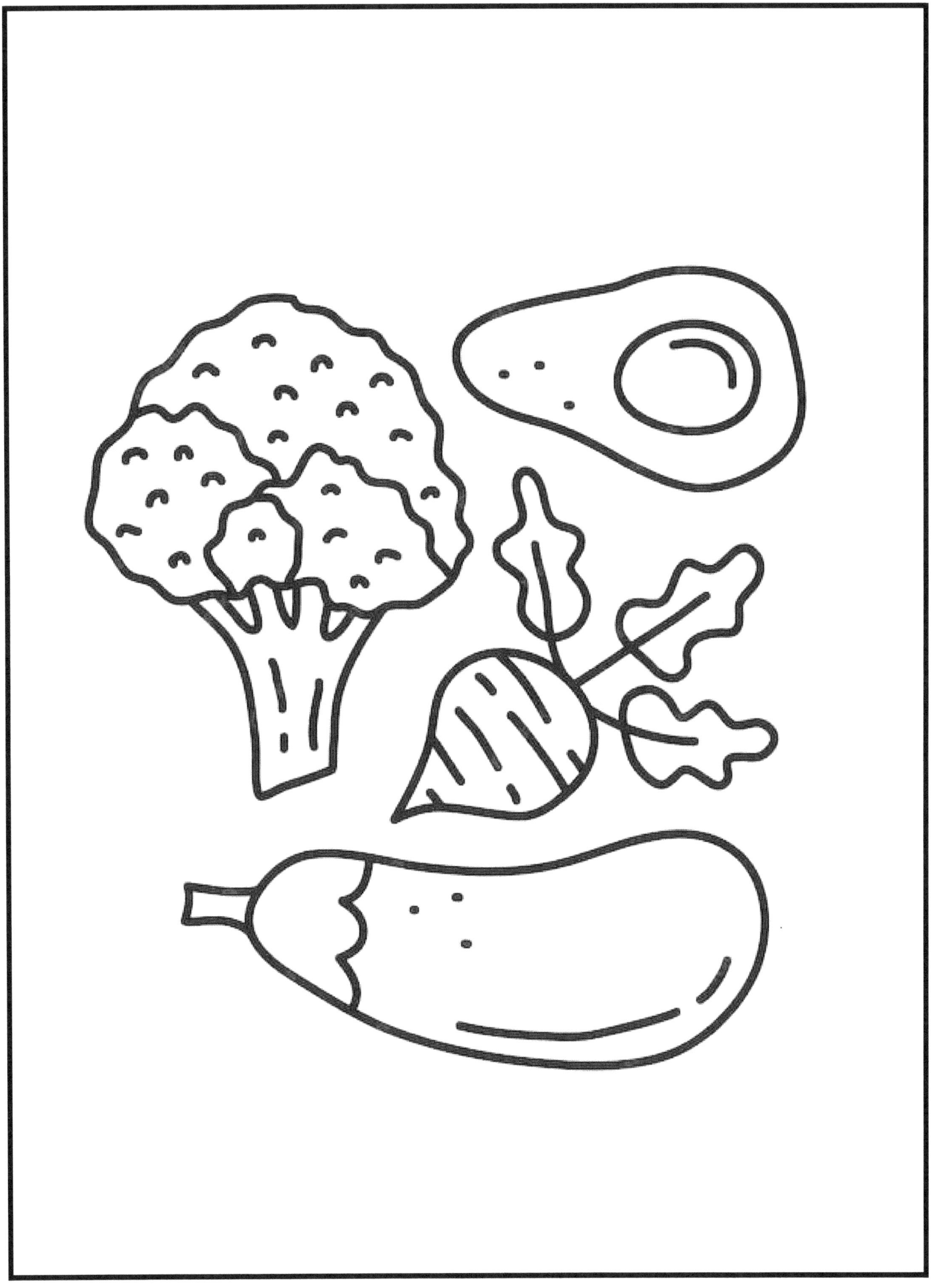

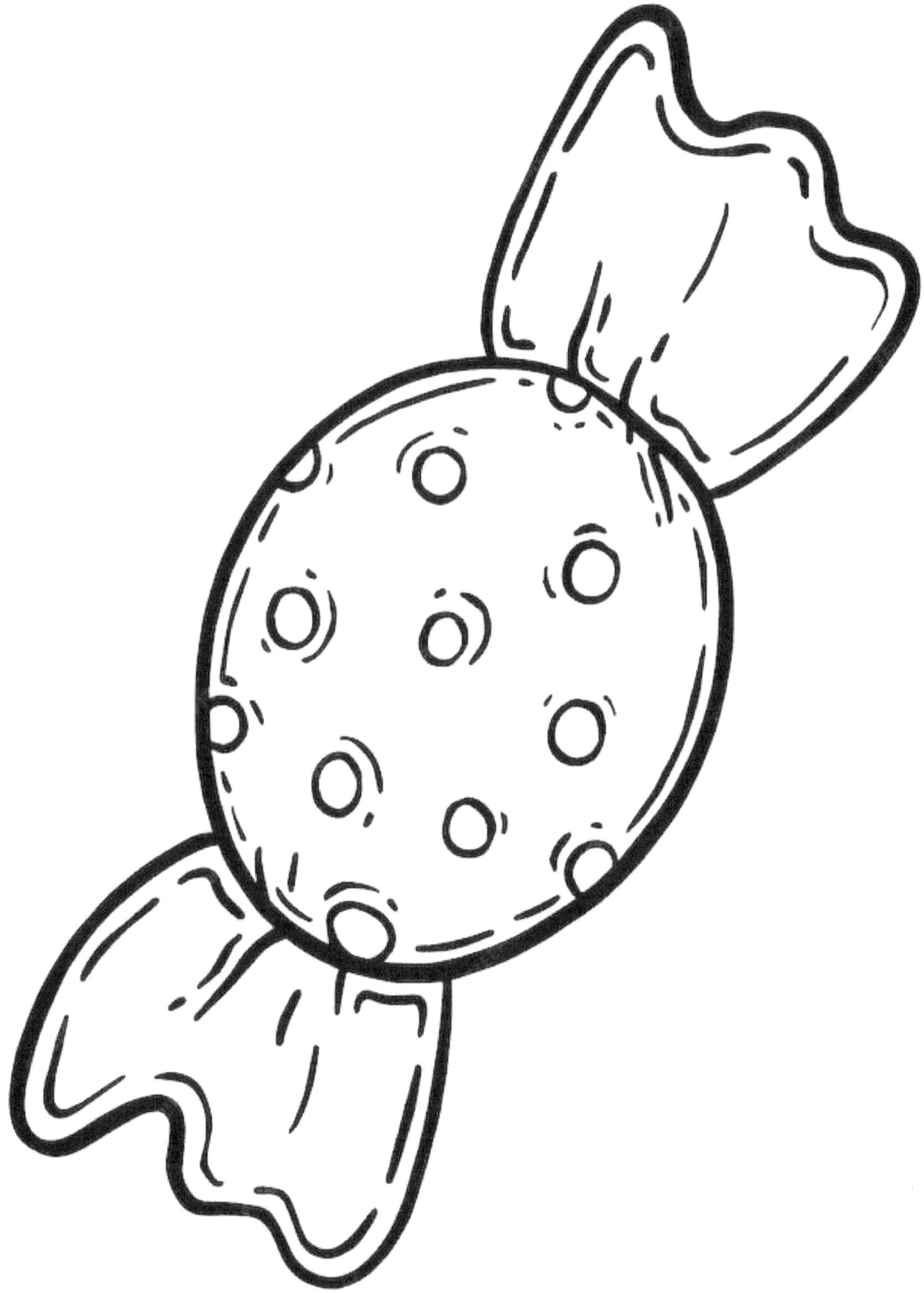

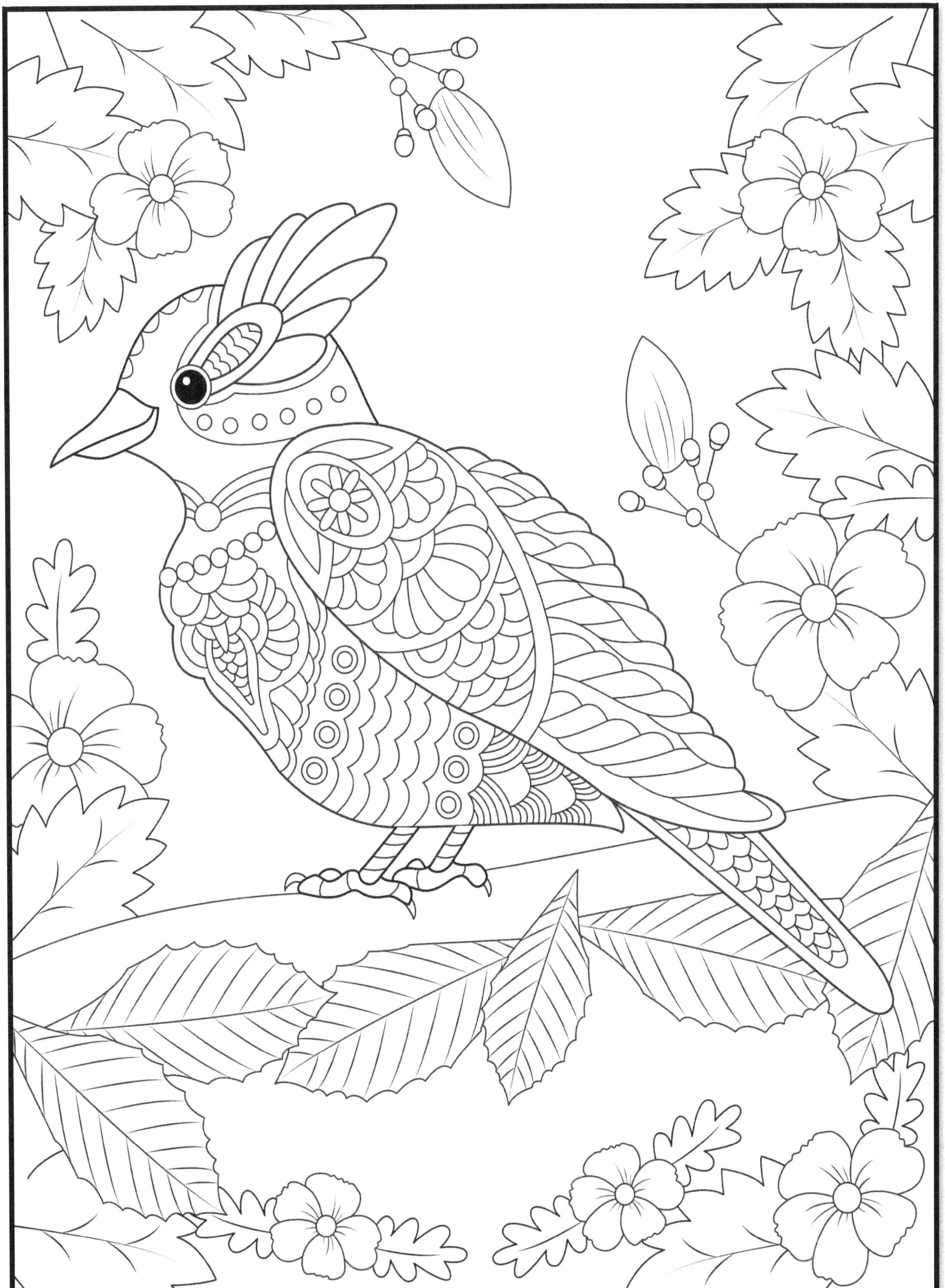

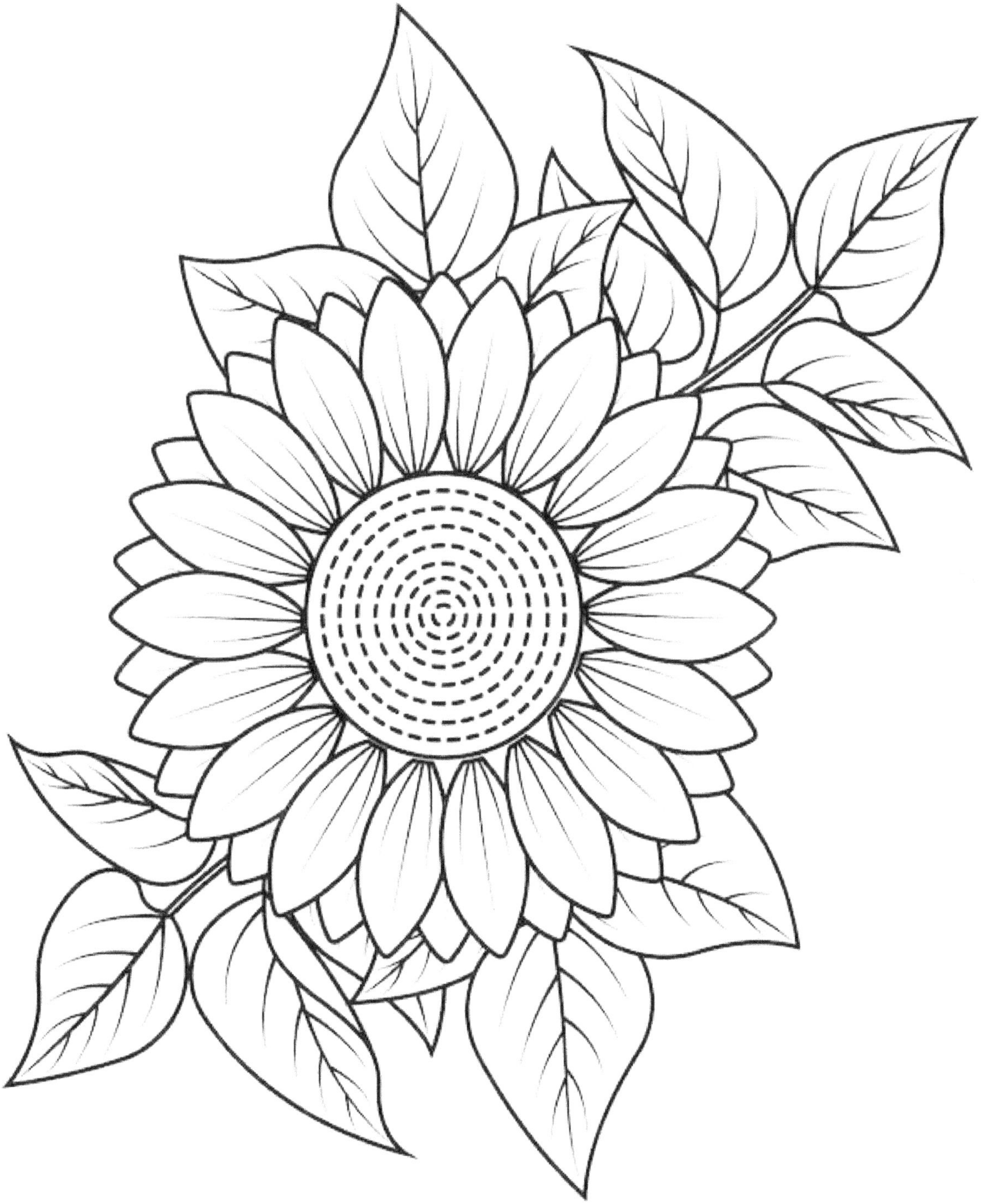

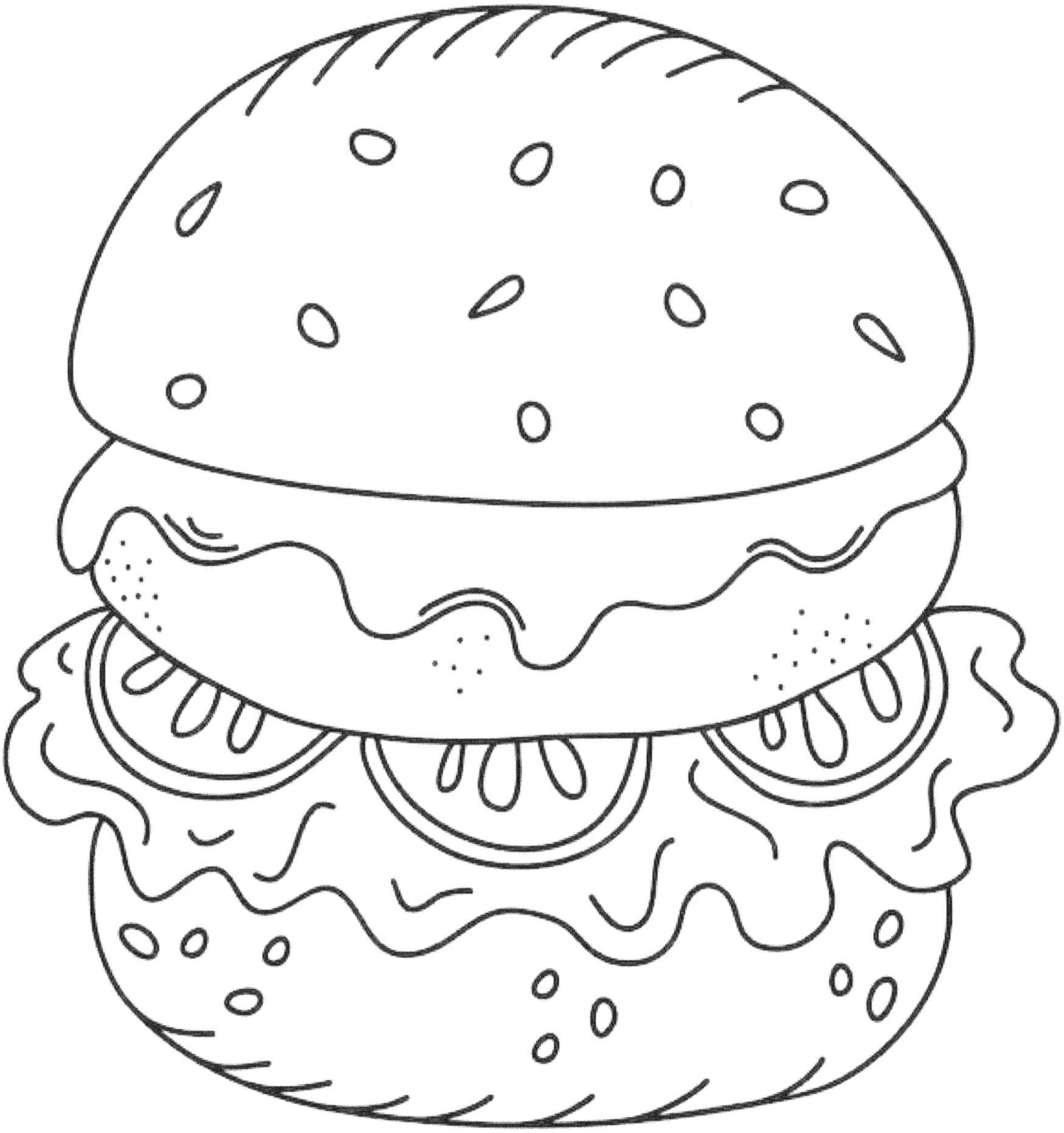

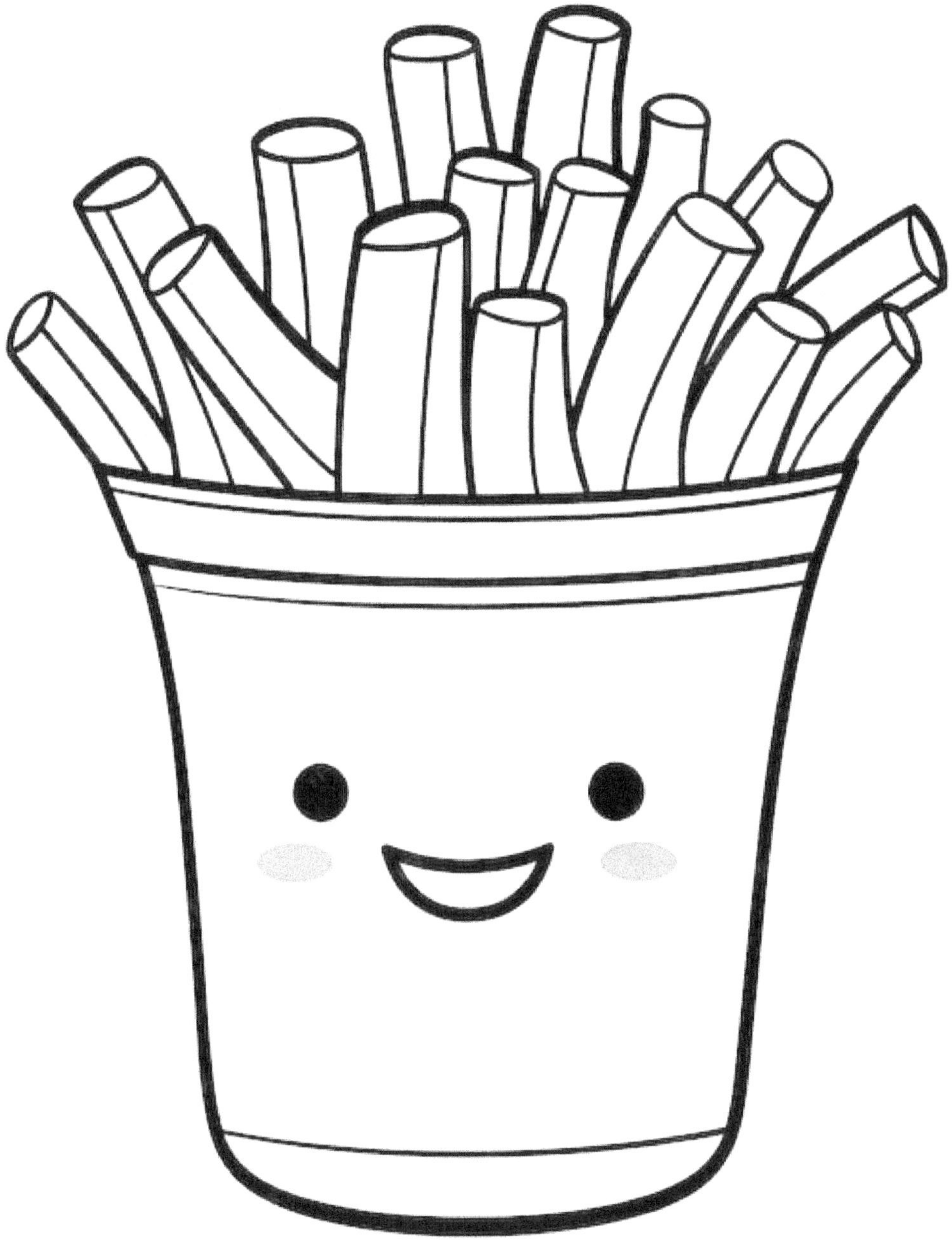

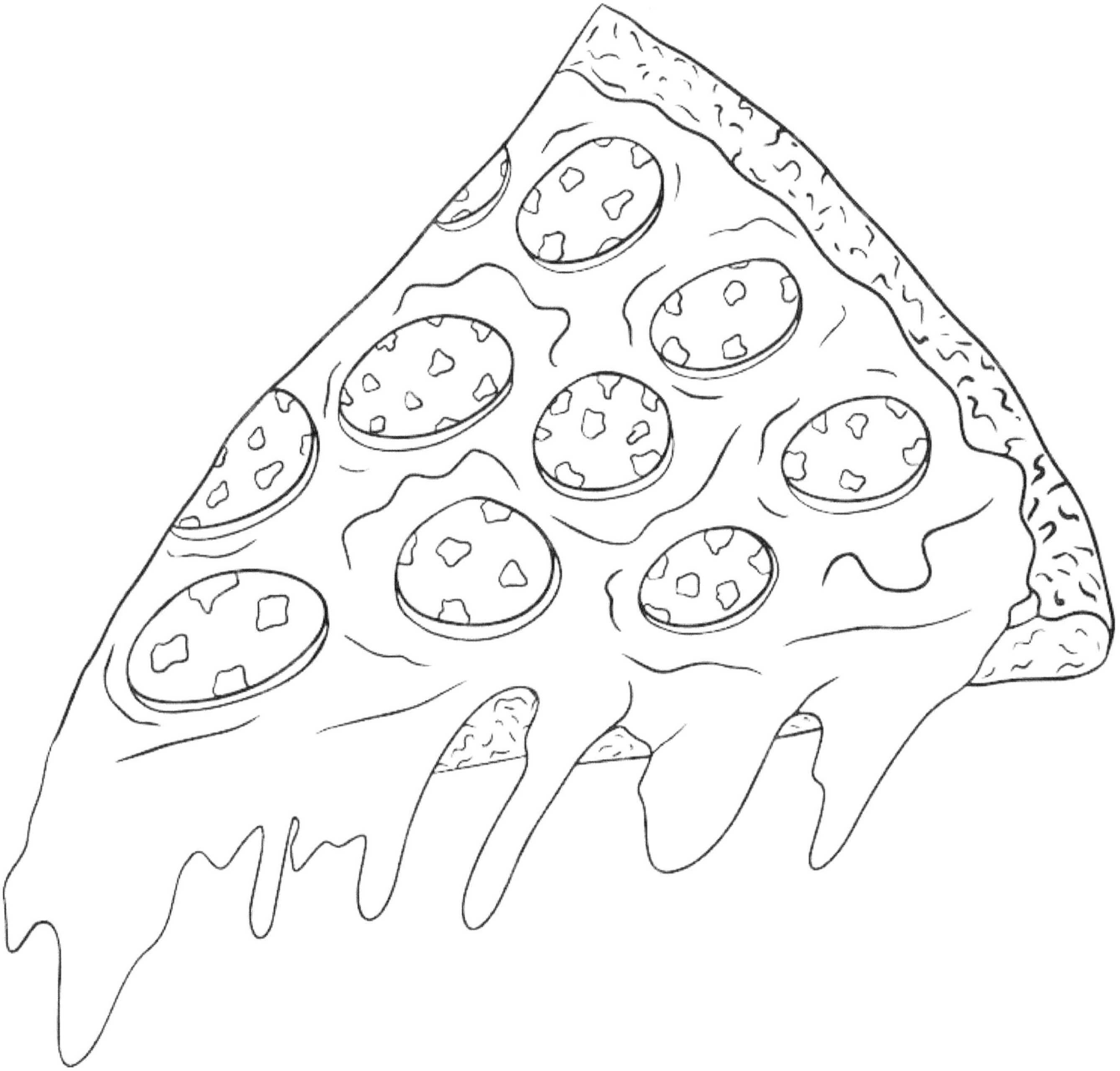

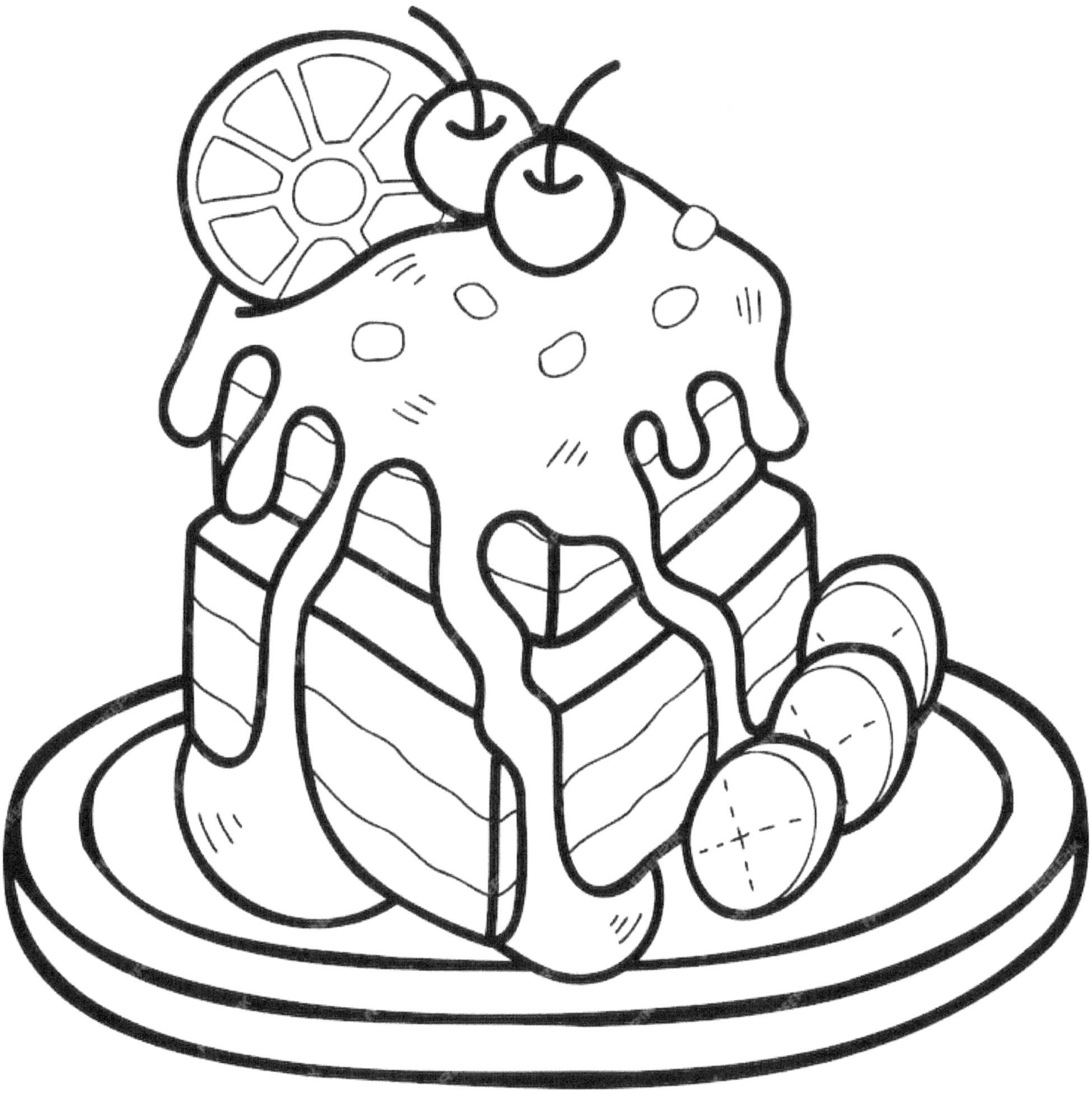

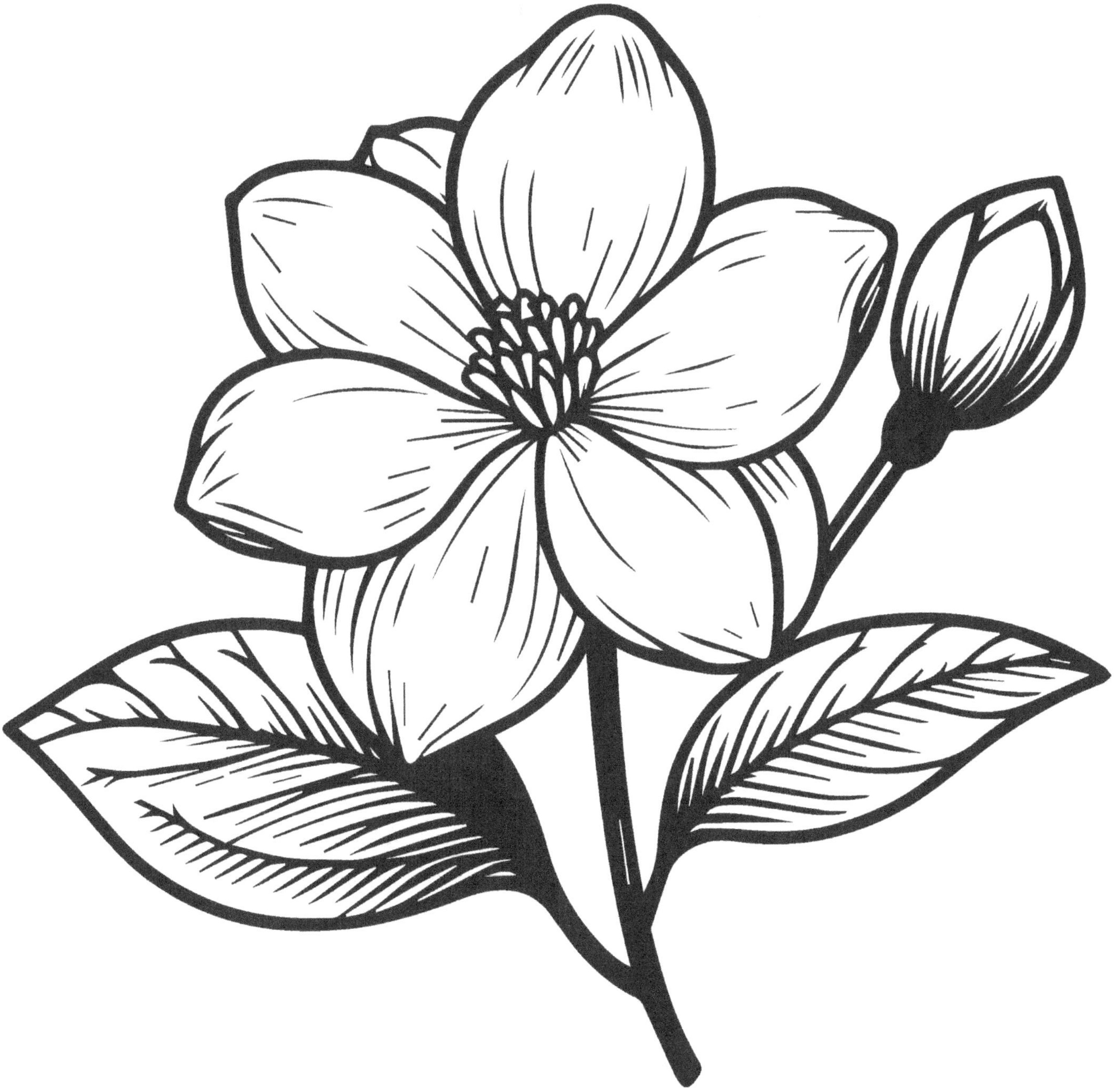

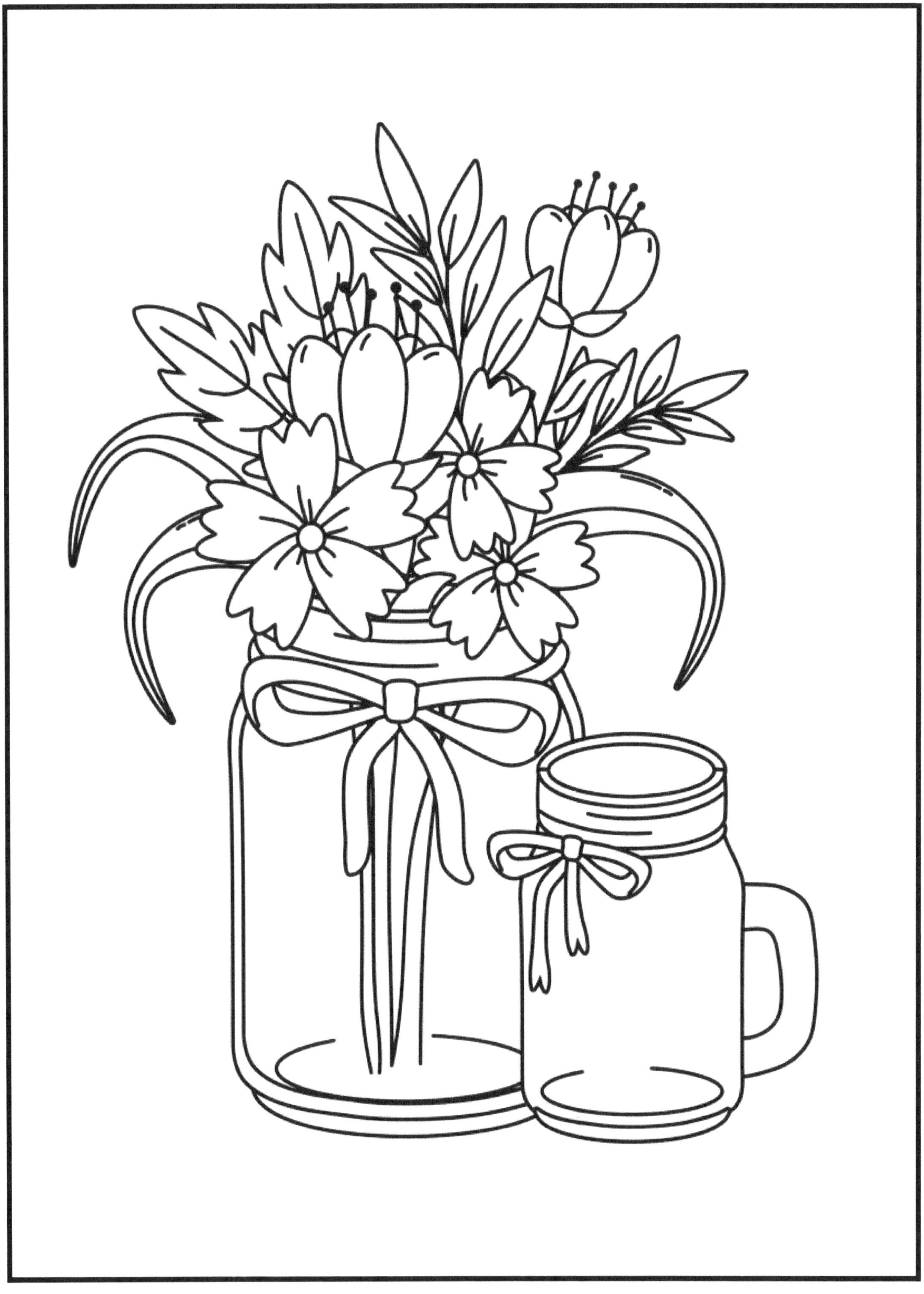

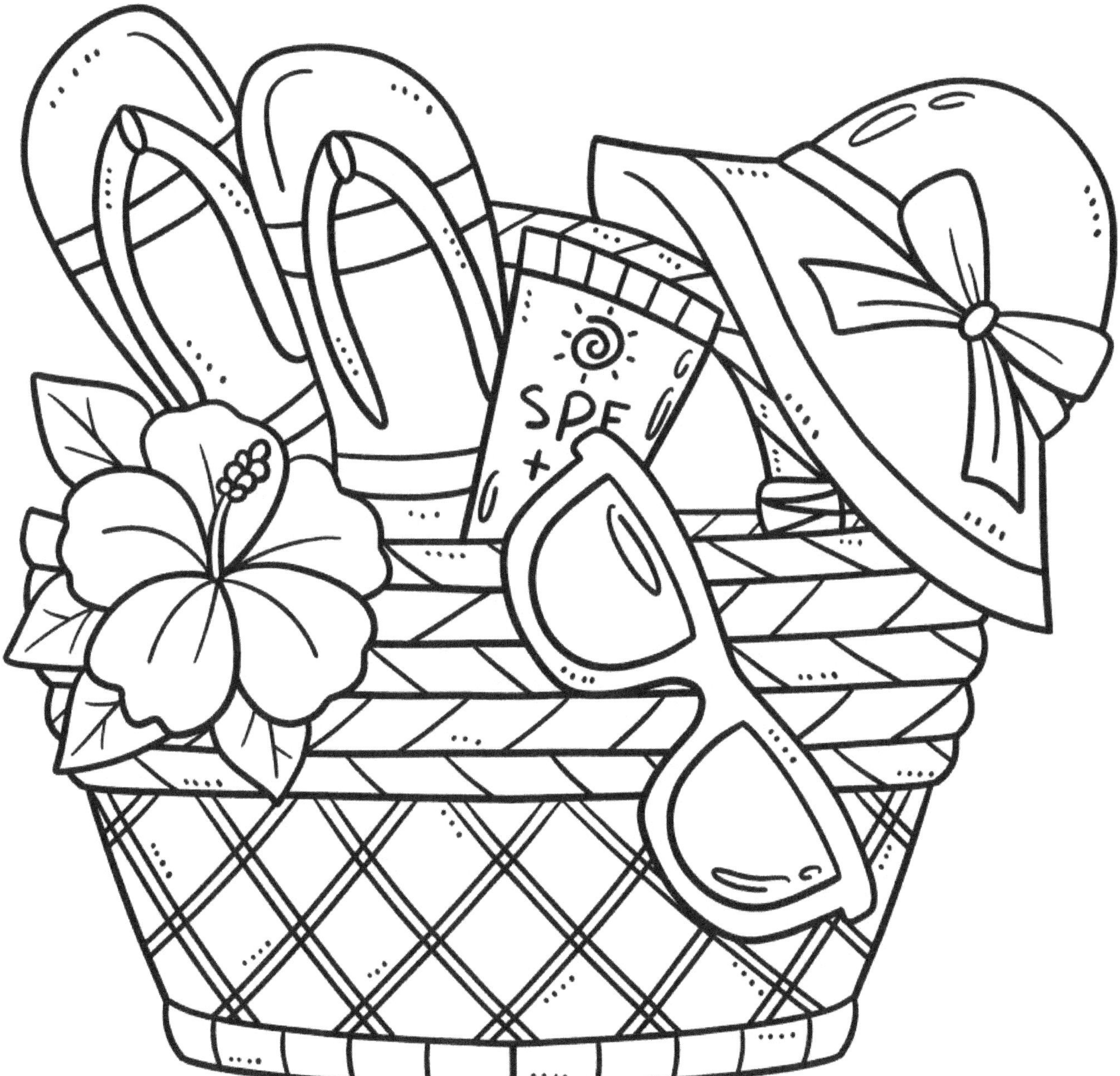
SPF

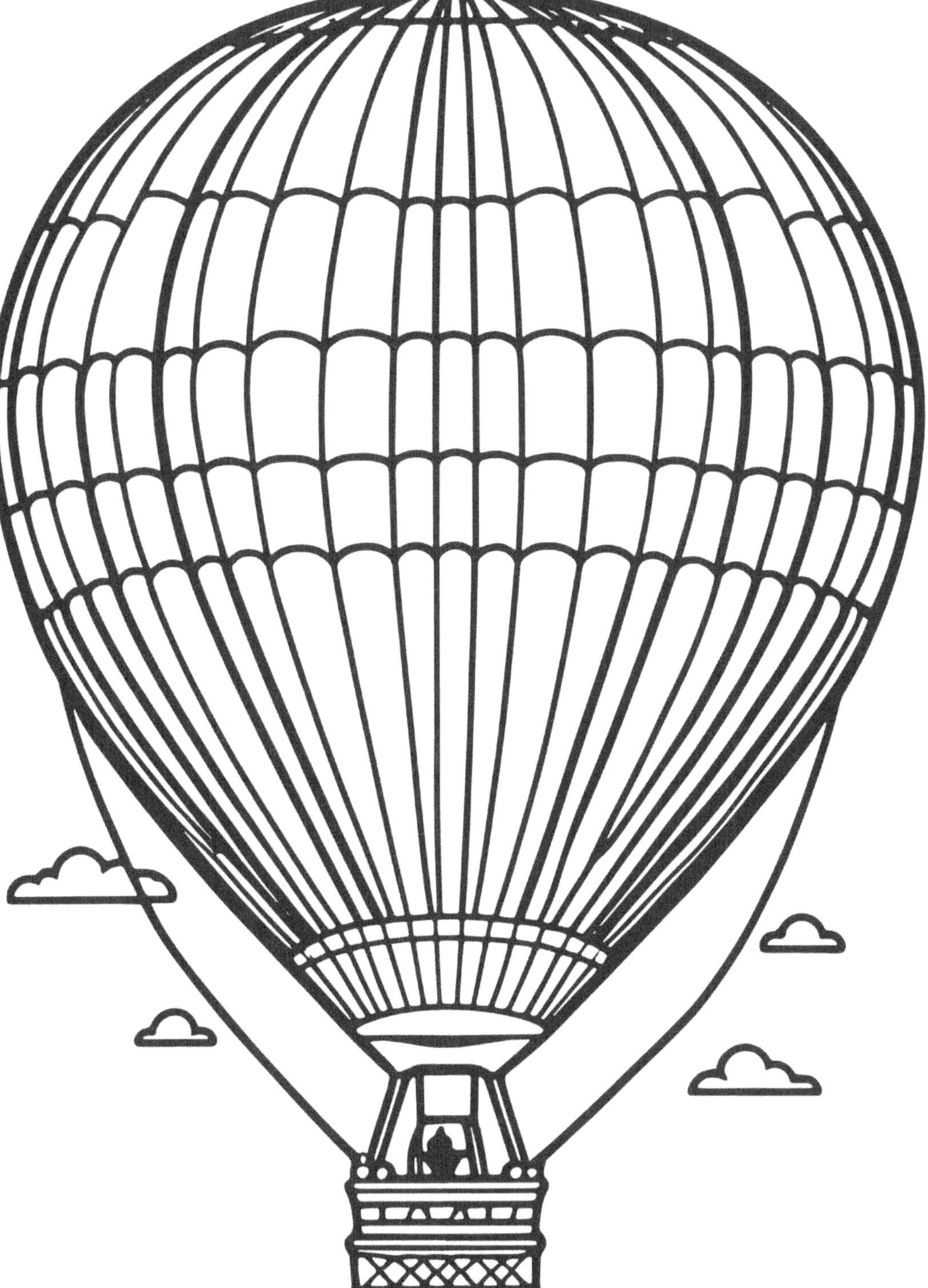

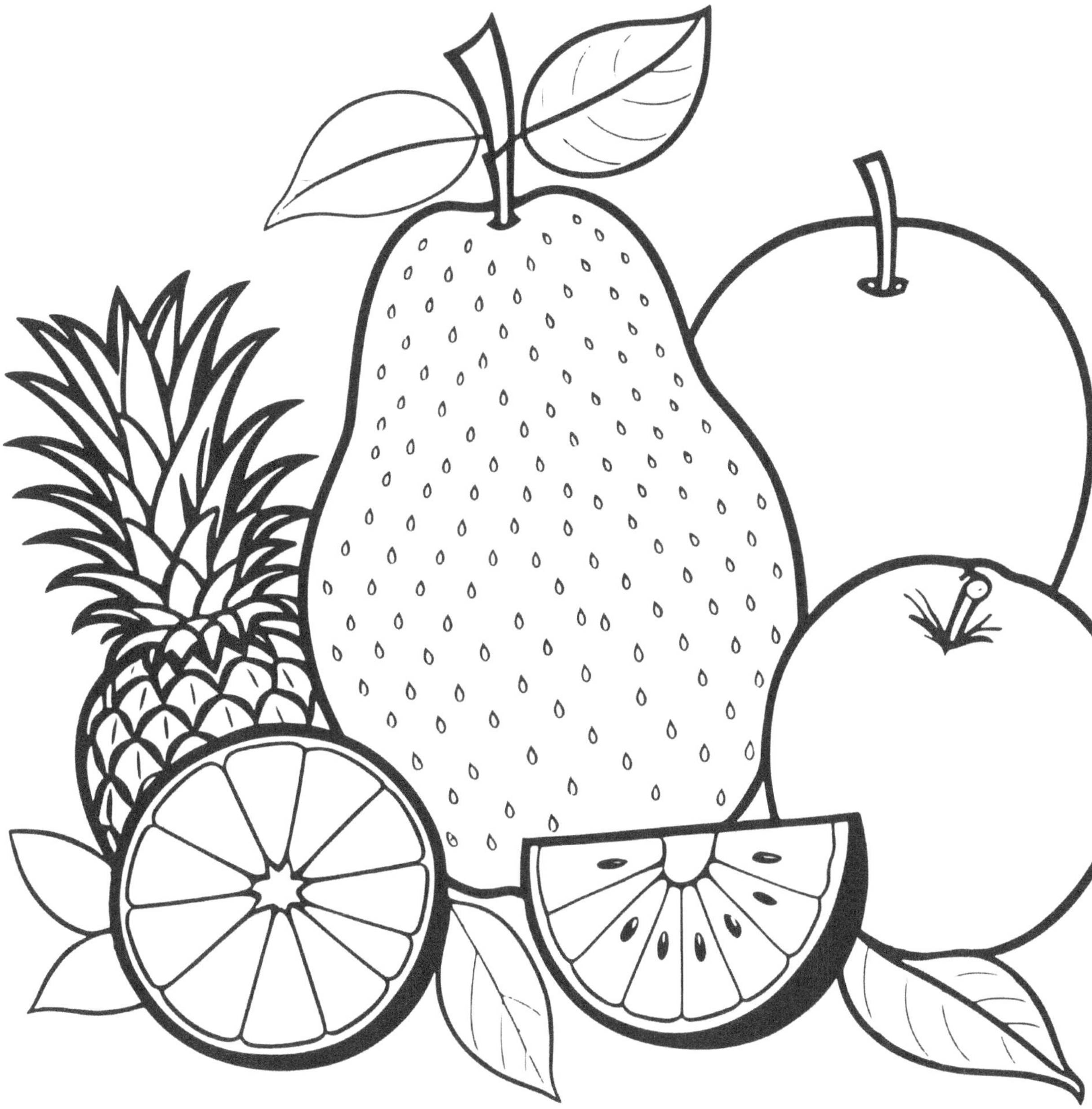

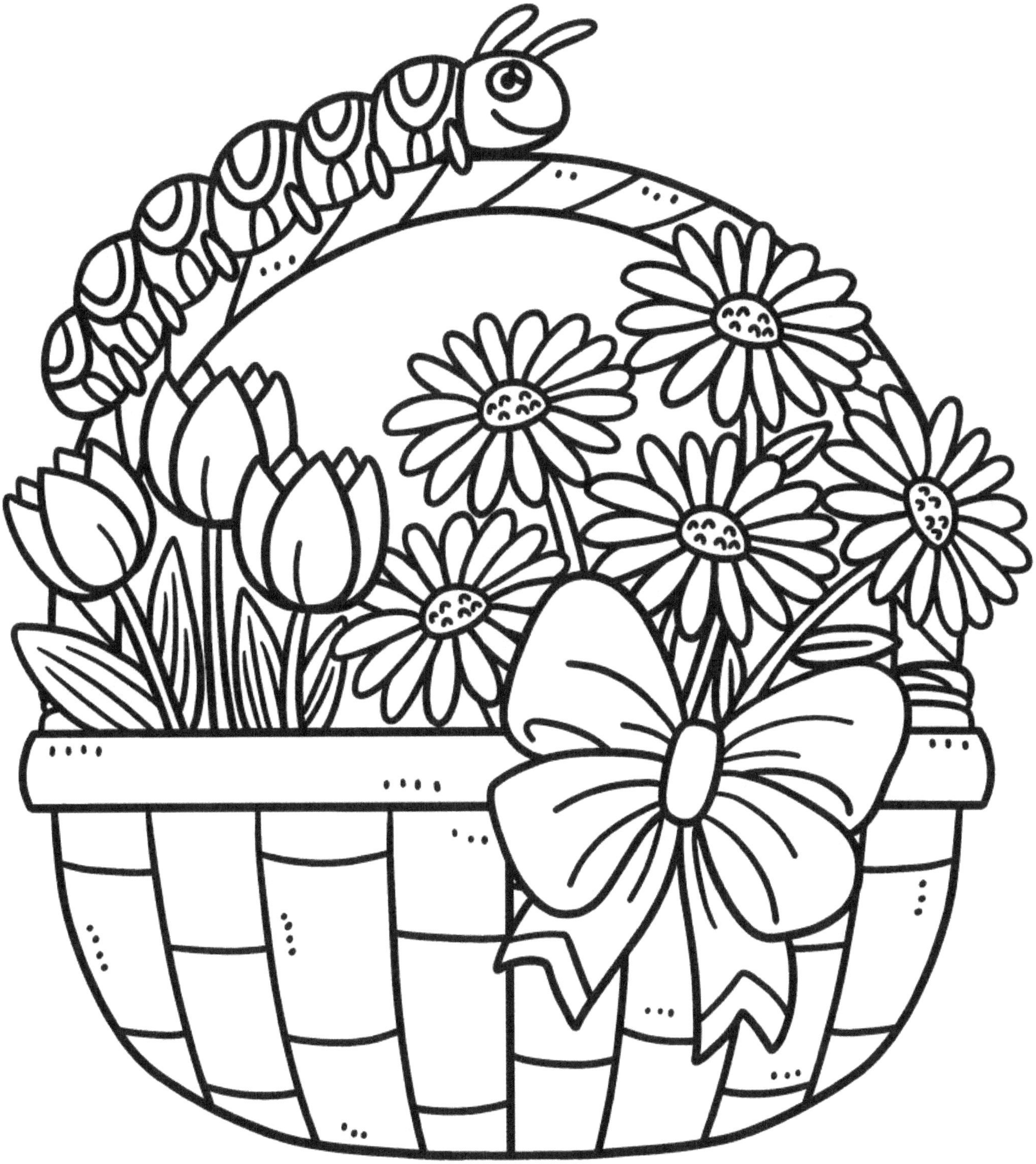

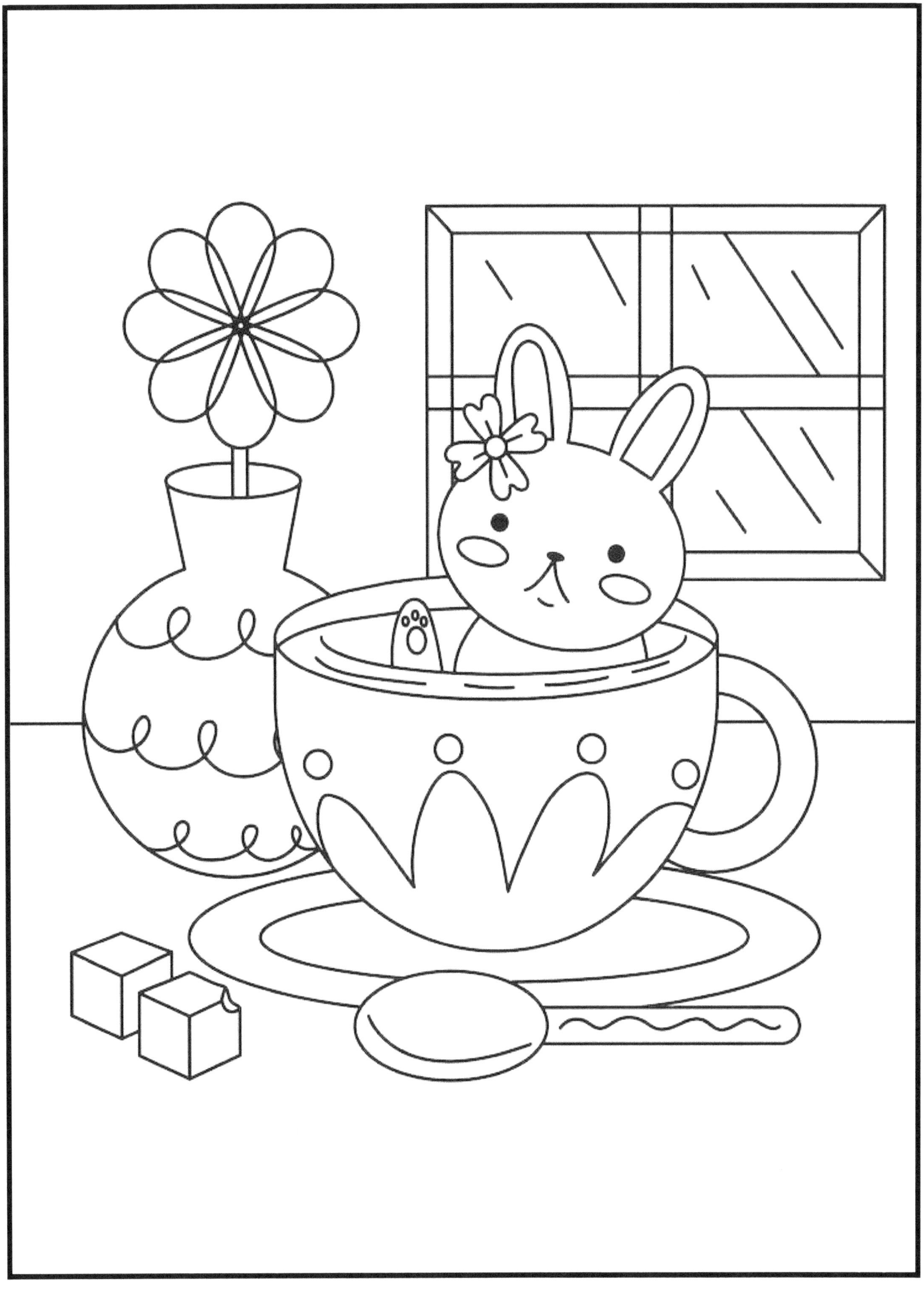

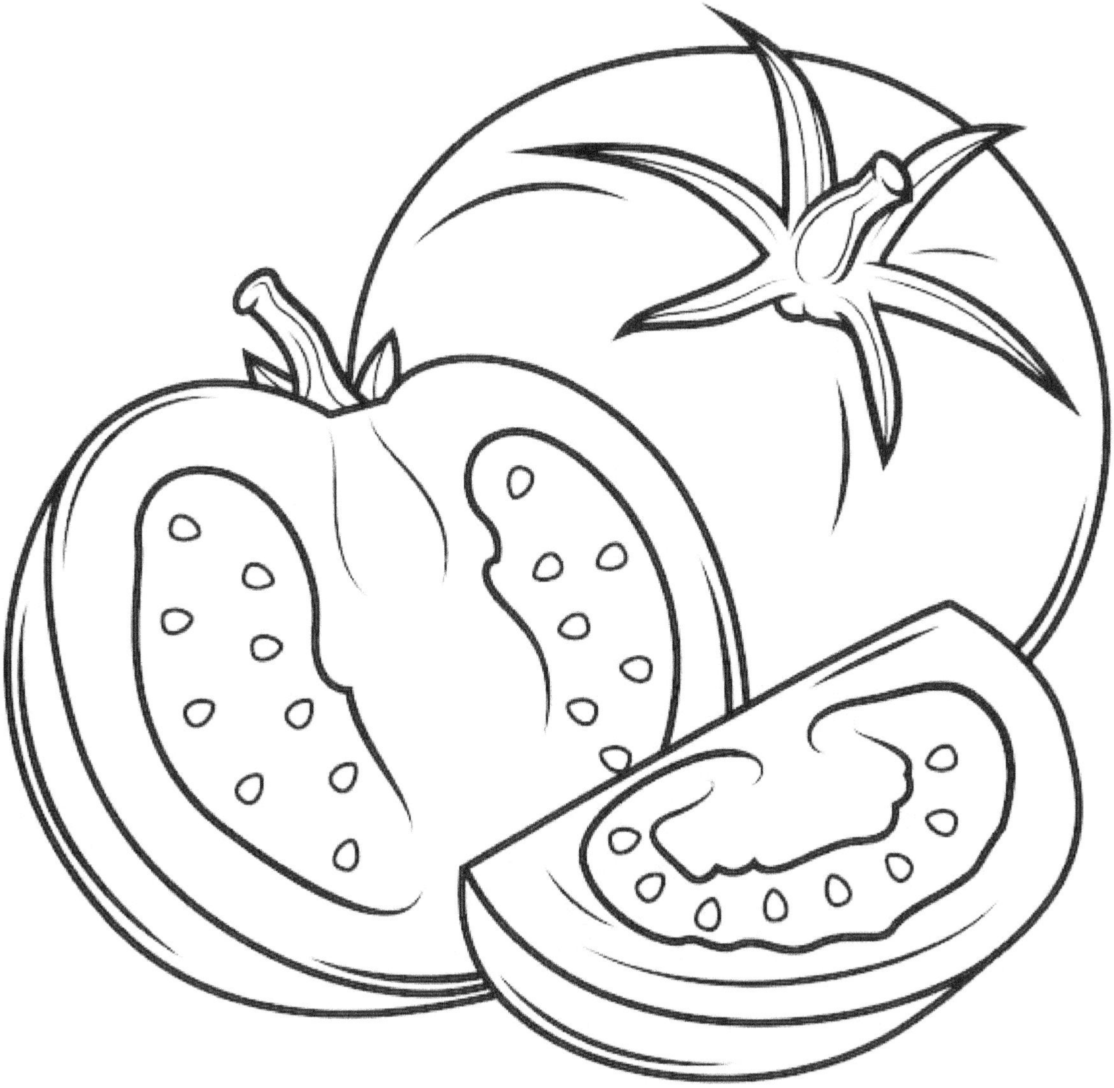

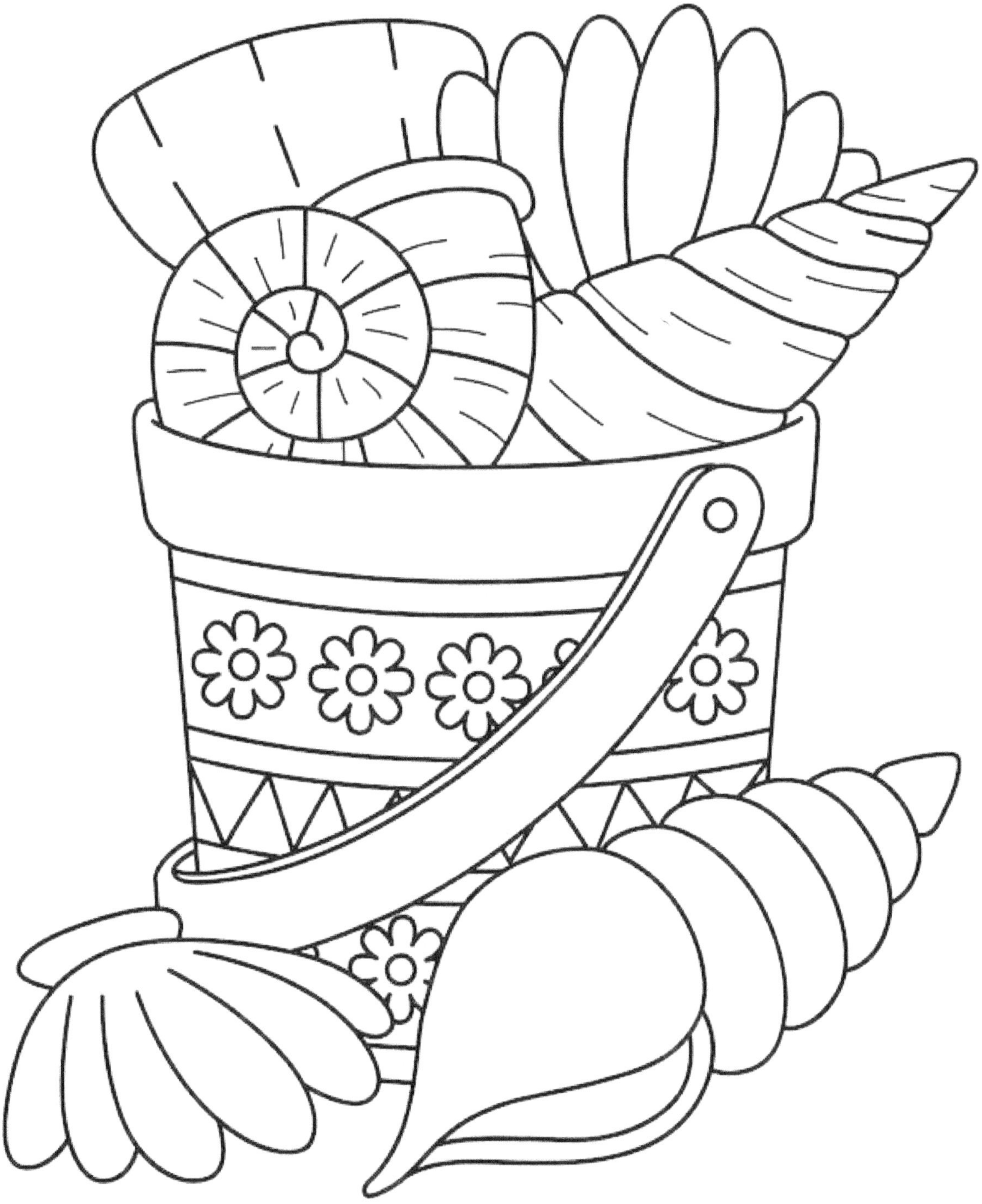

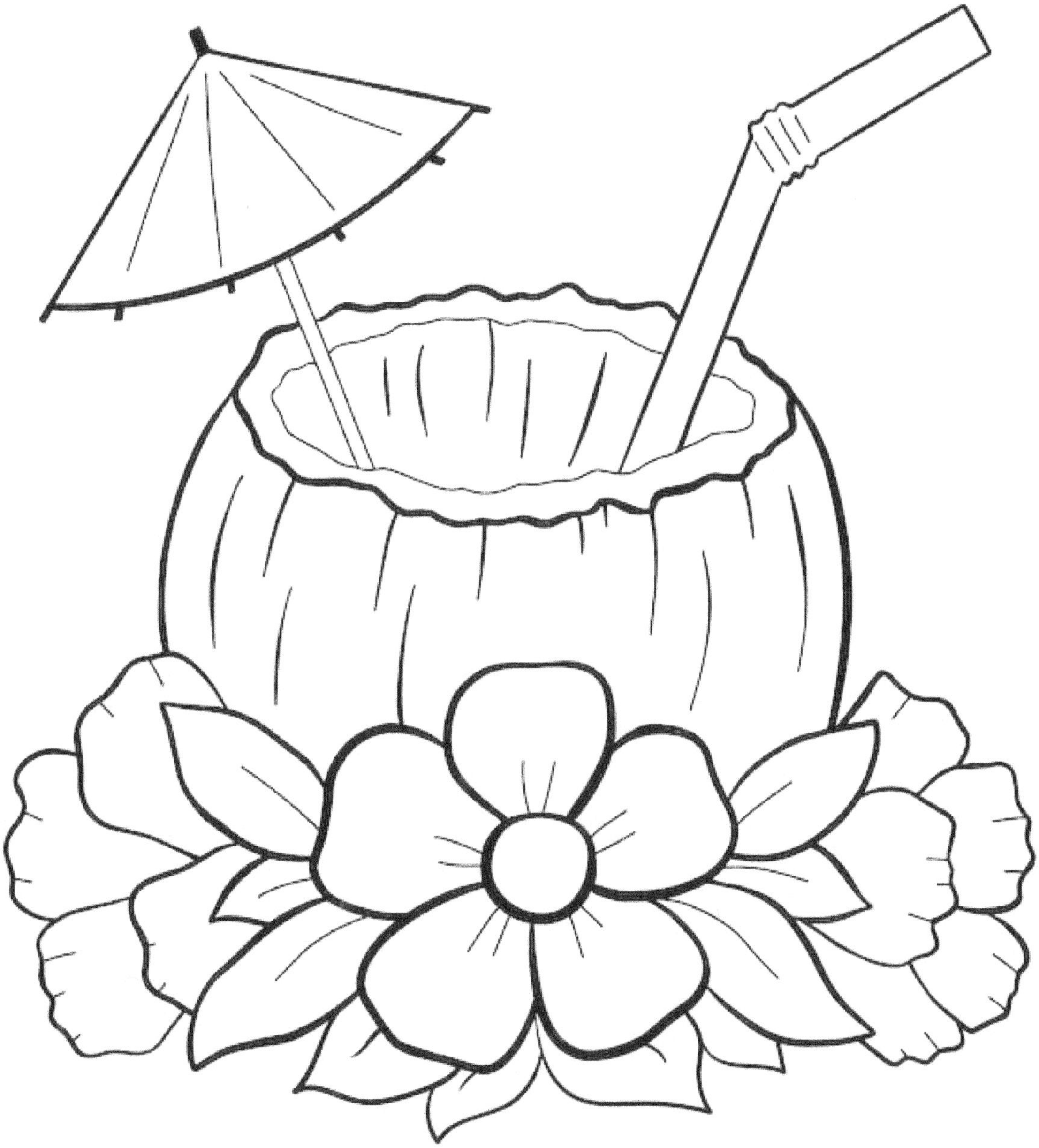

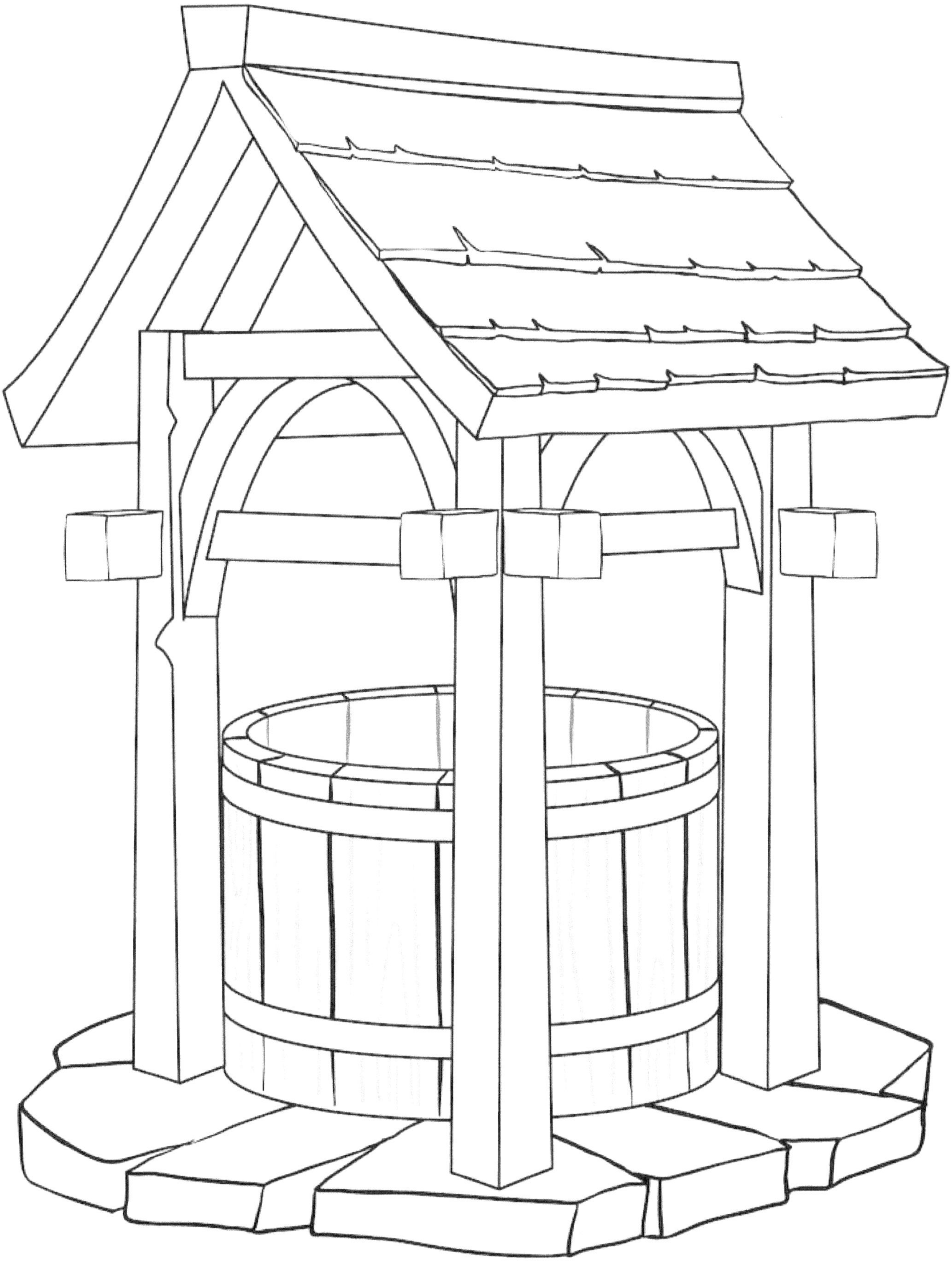

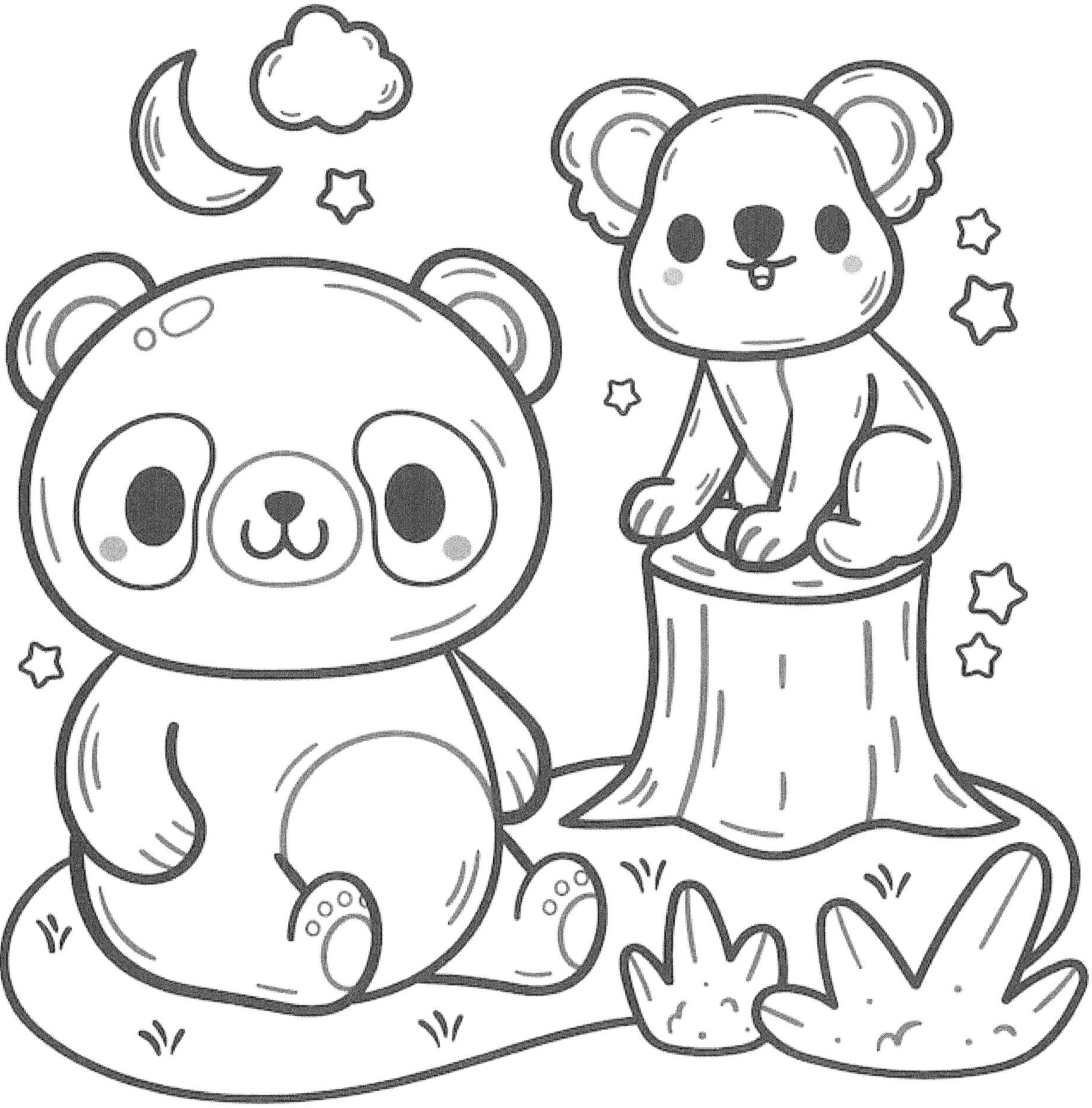

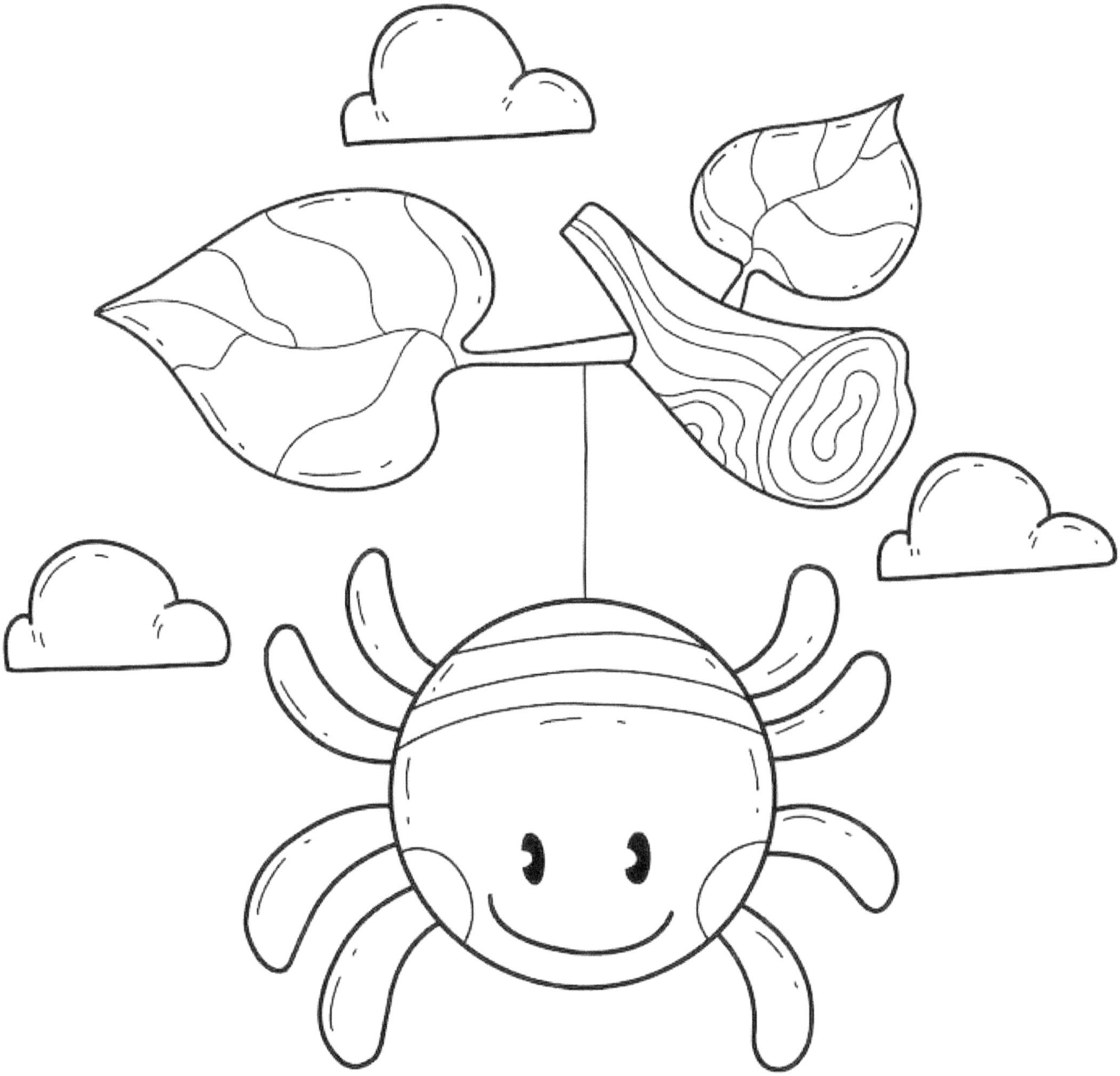

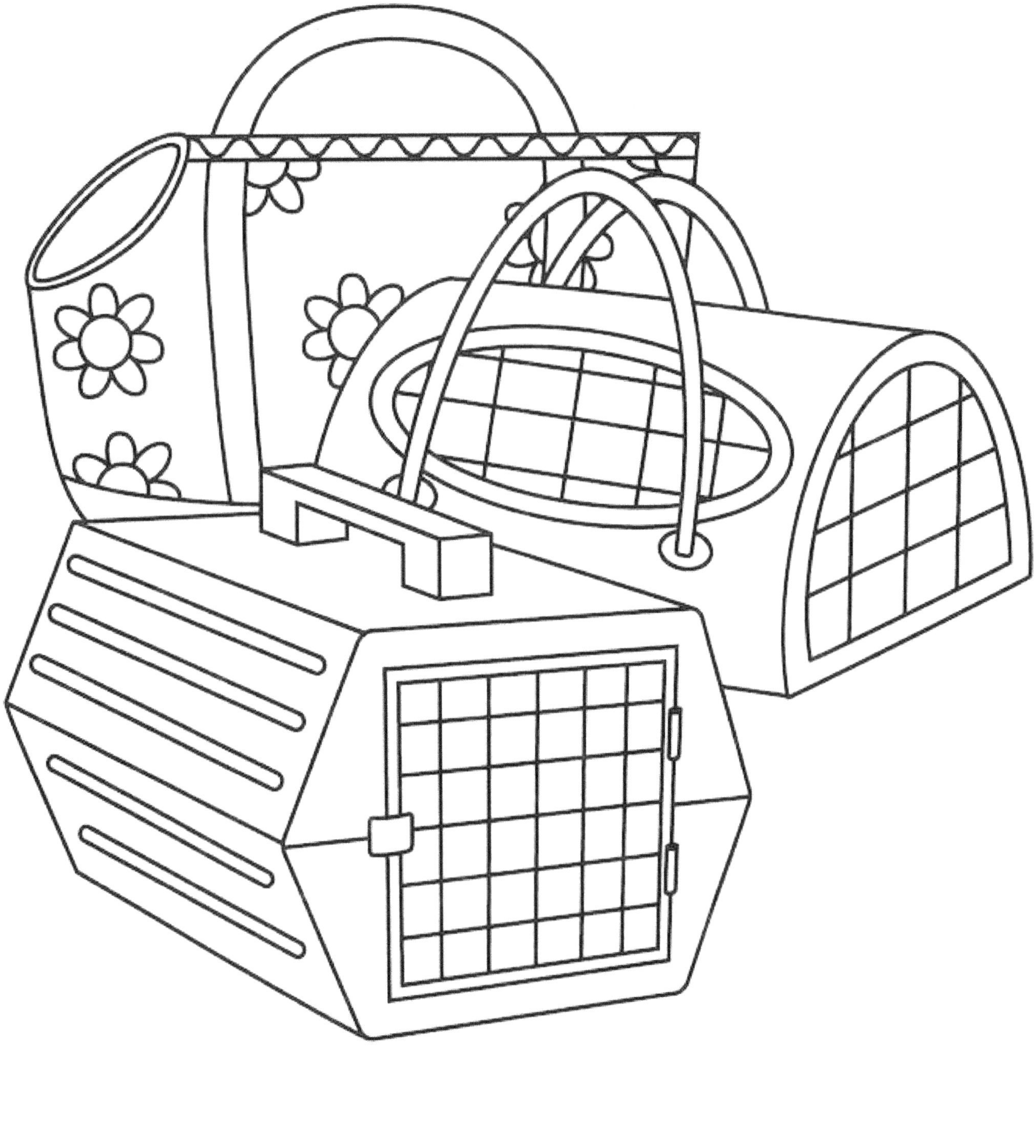

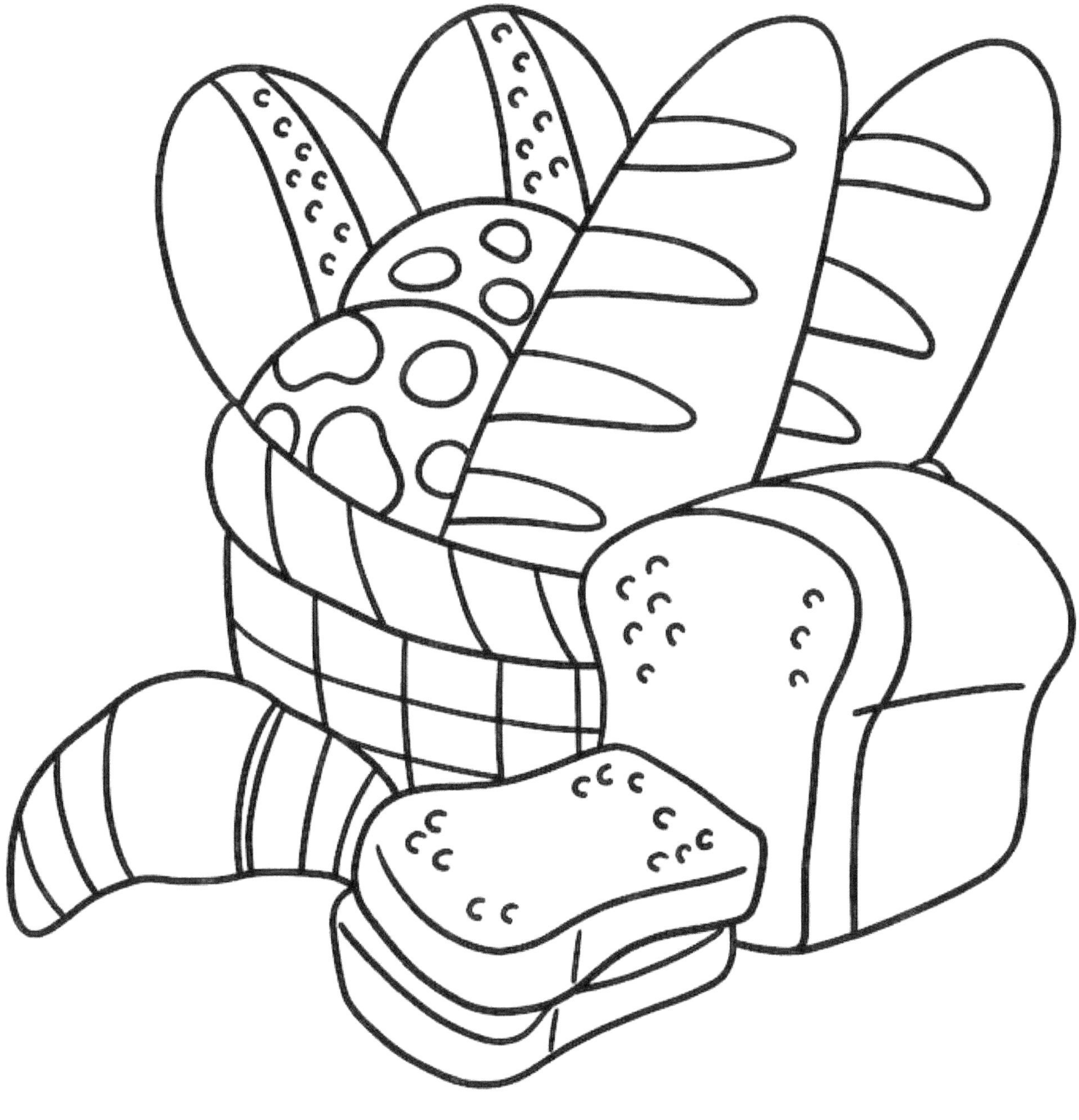

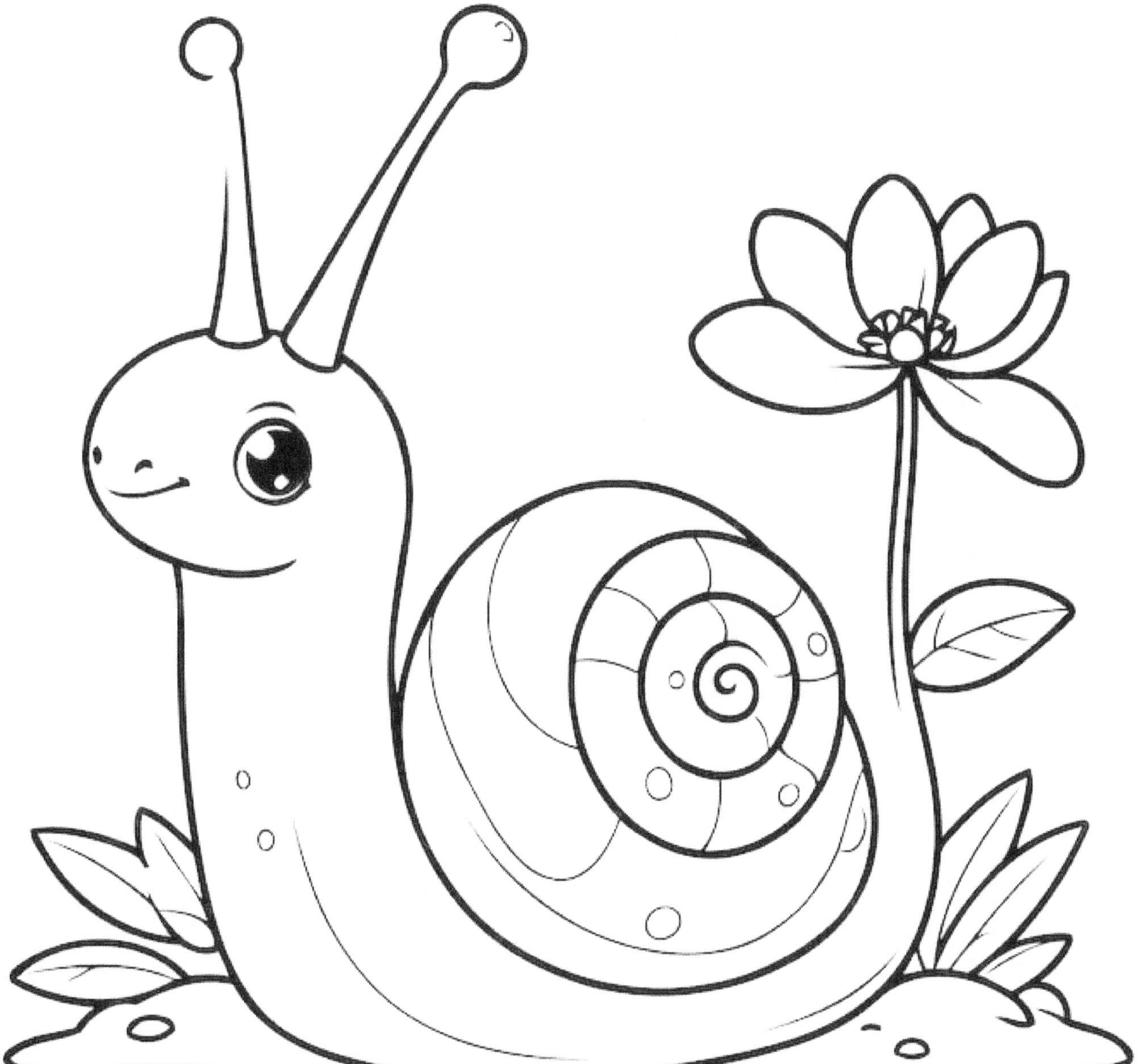

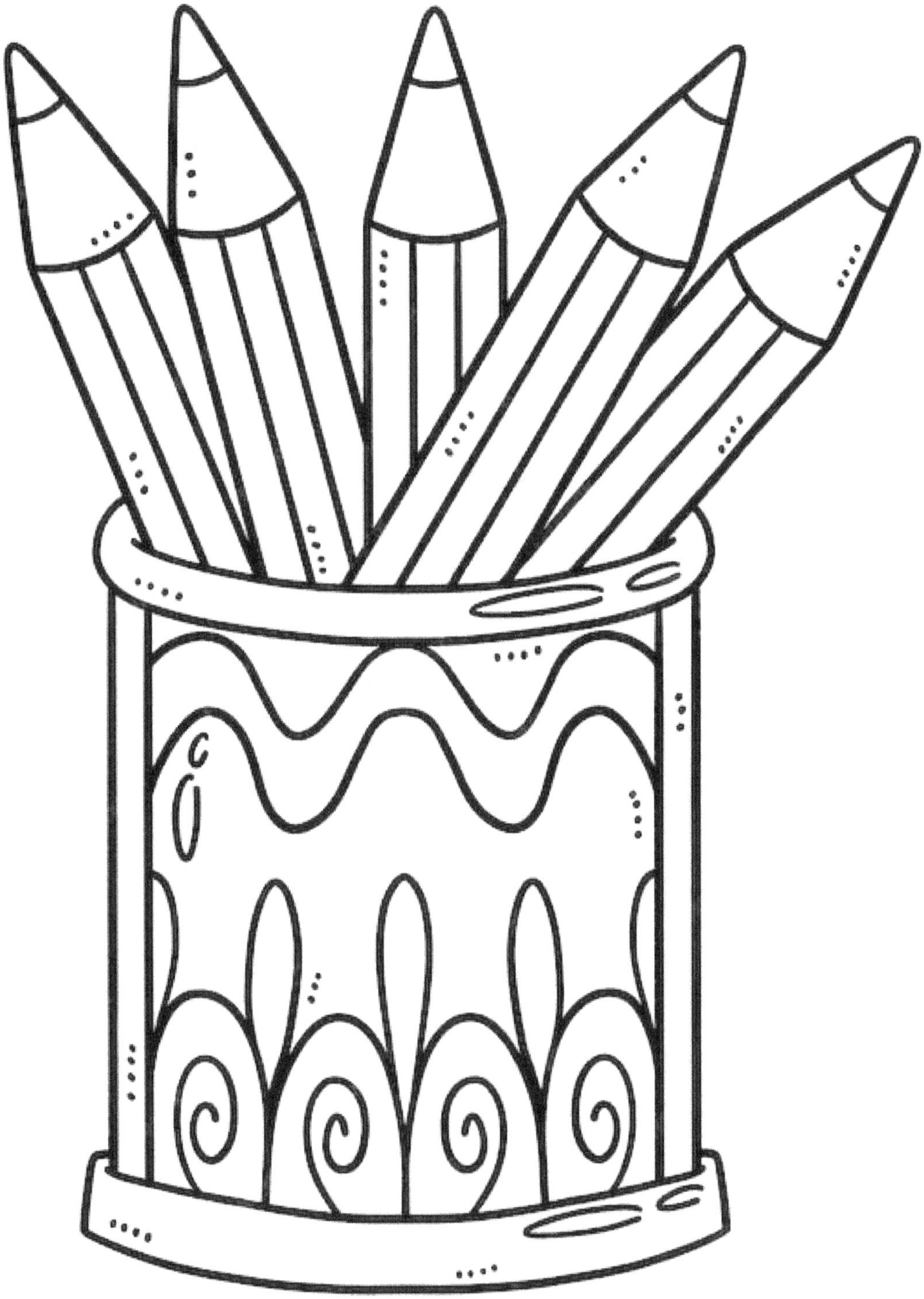

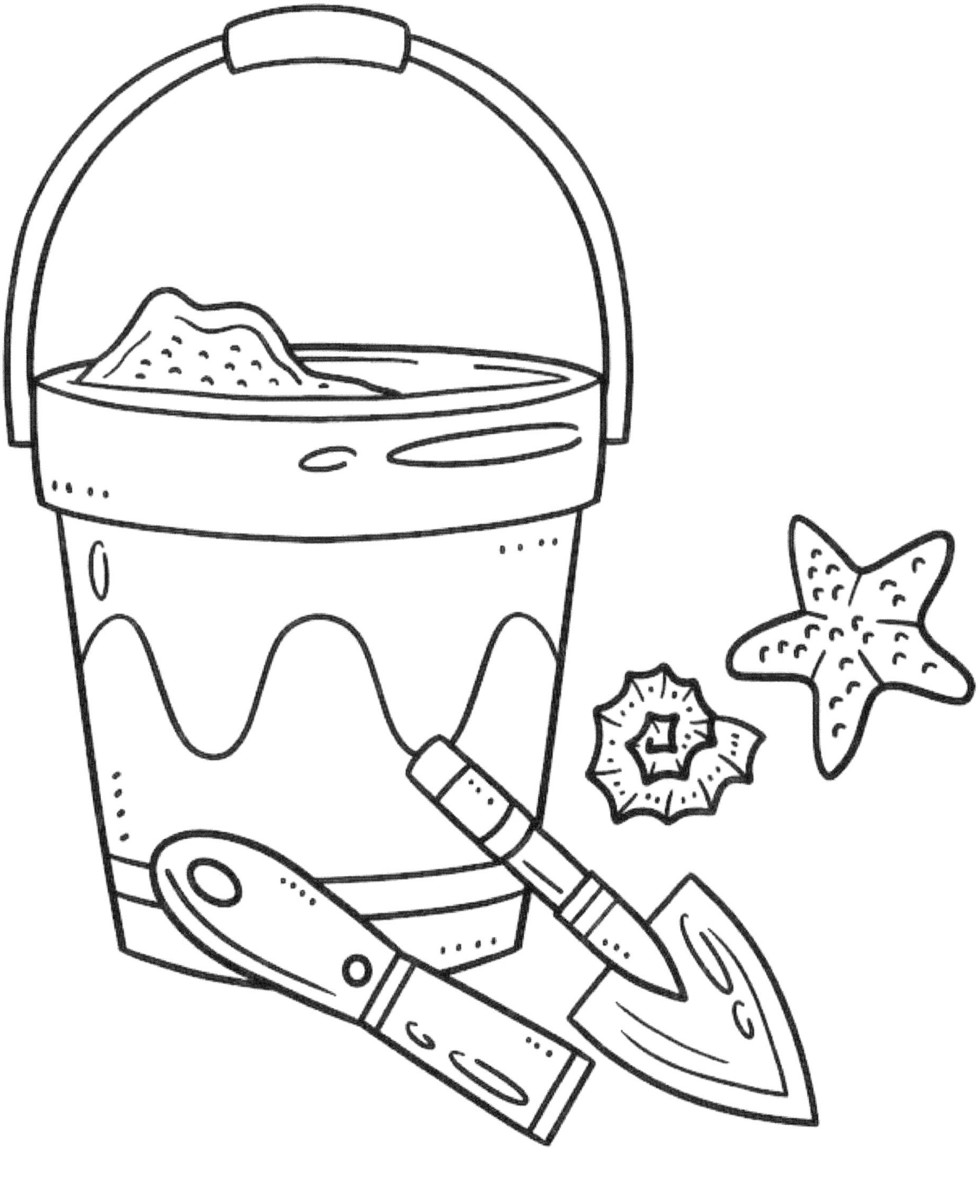

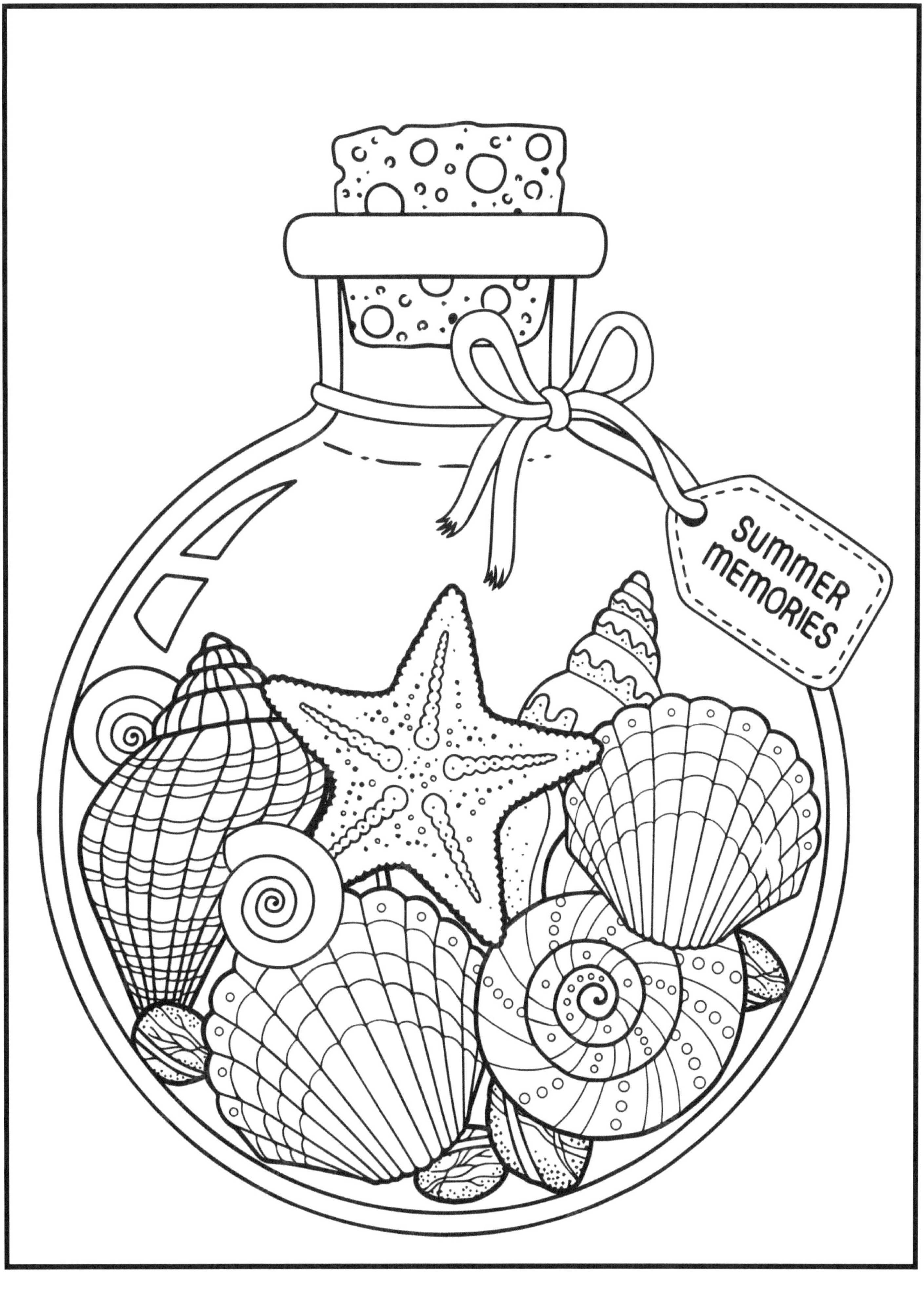
SUMMER MEMORIES

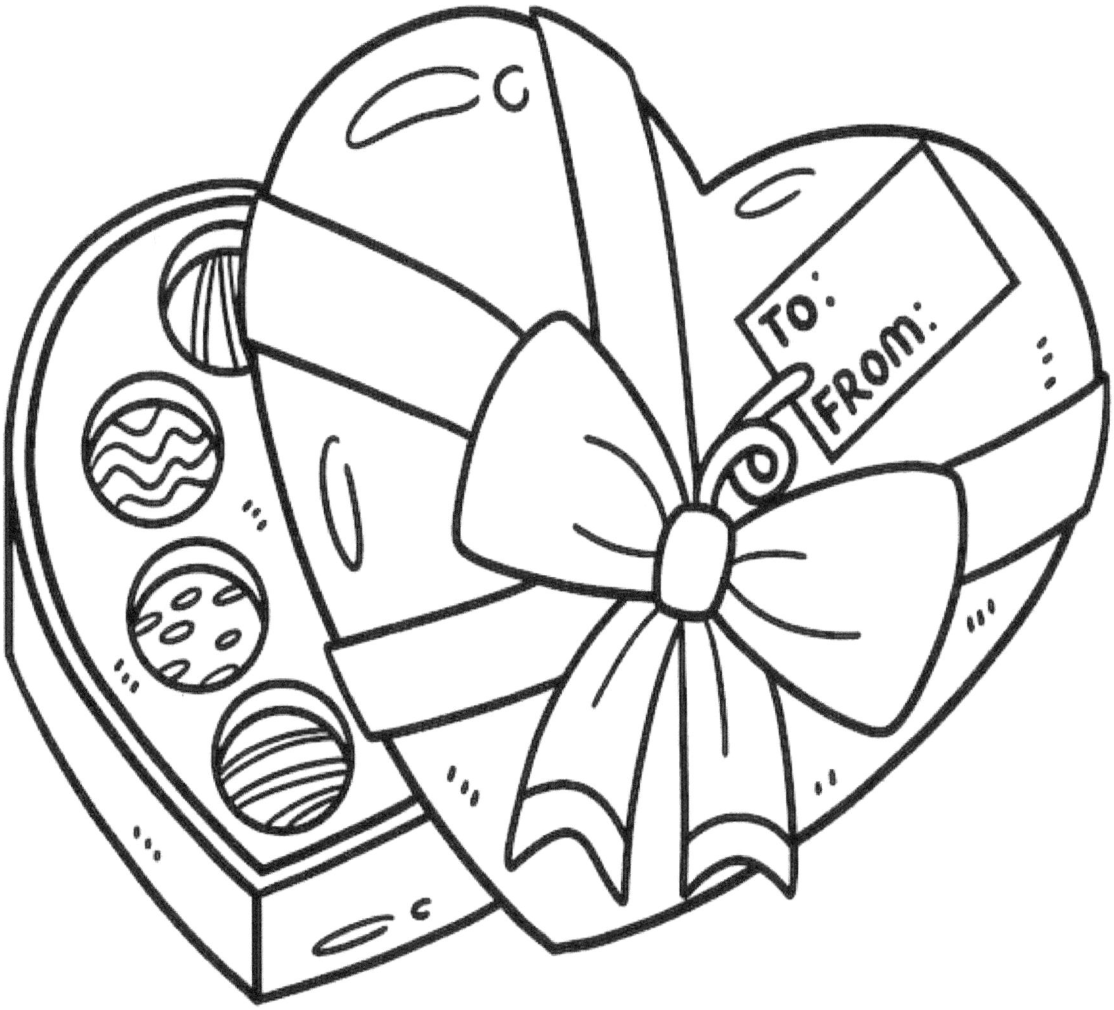
TO:
FROM:

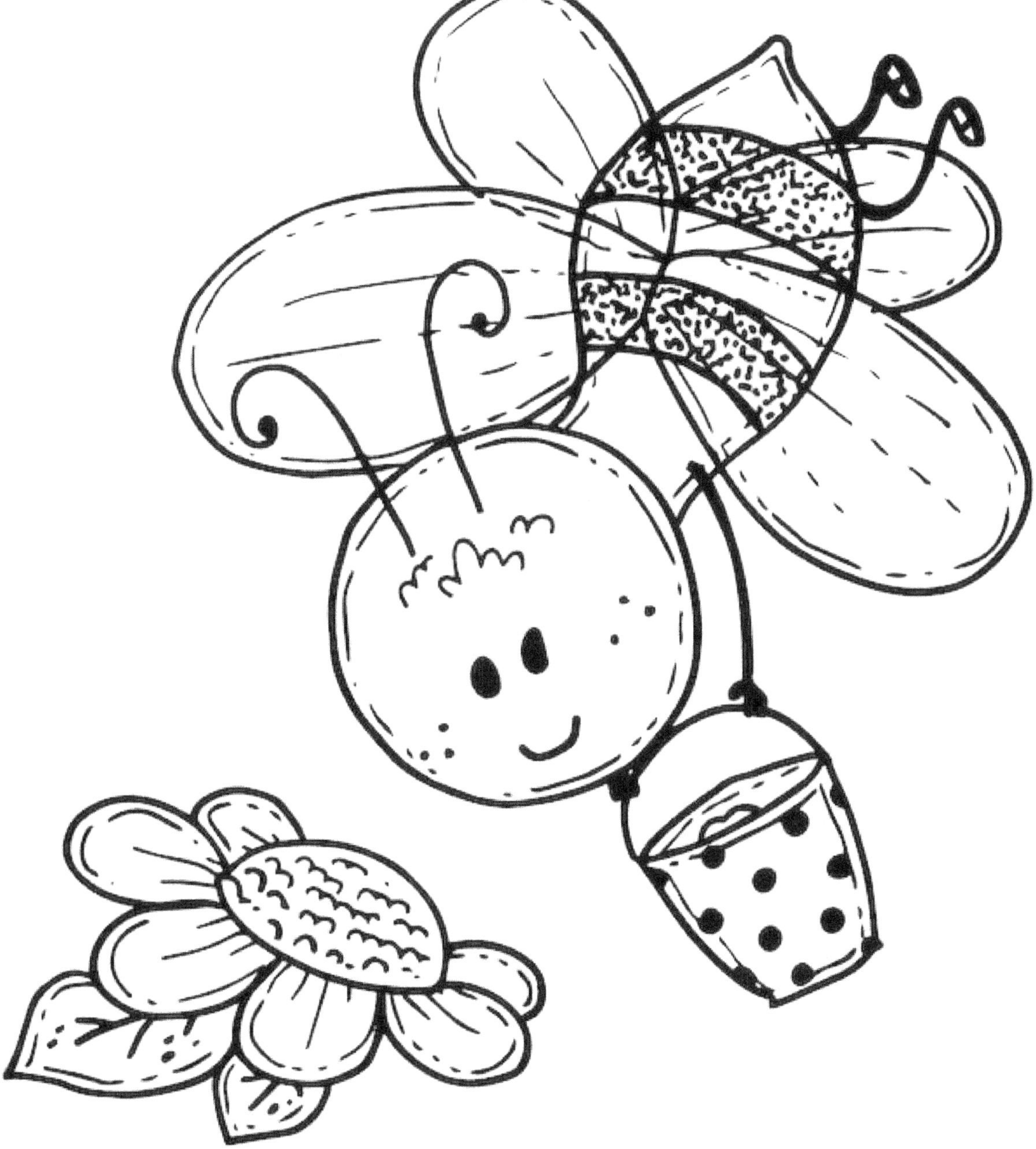

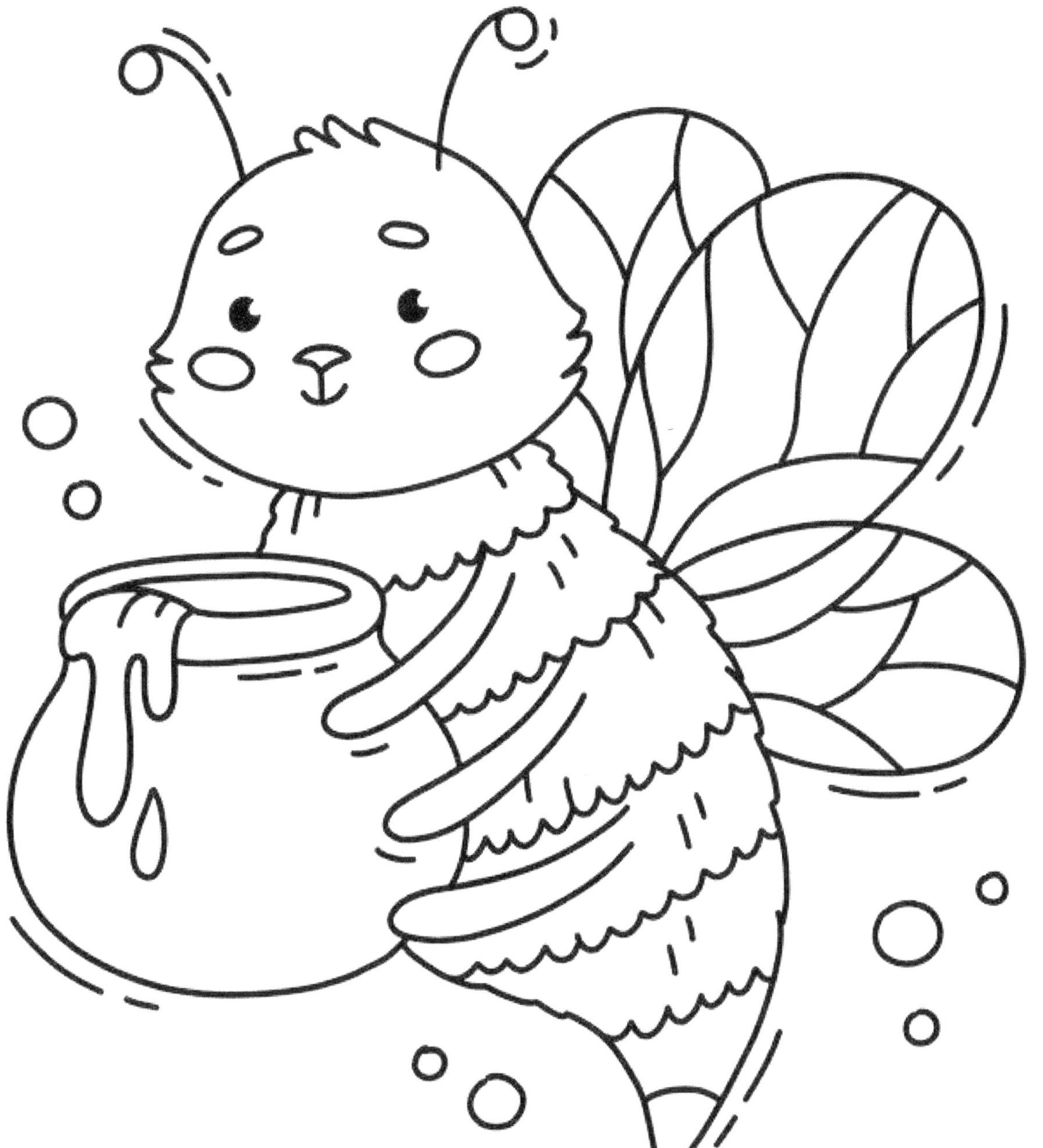

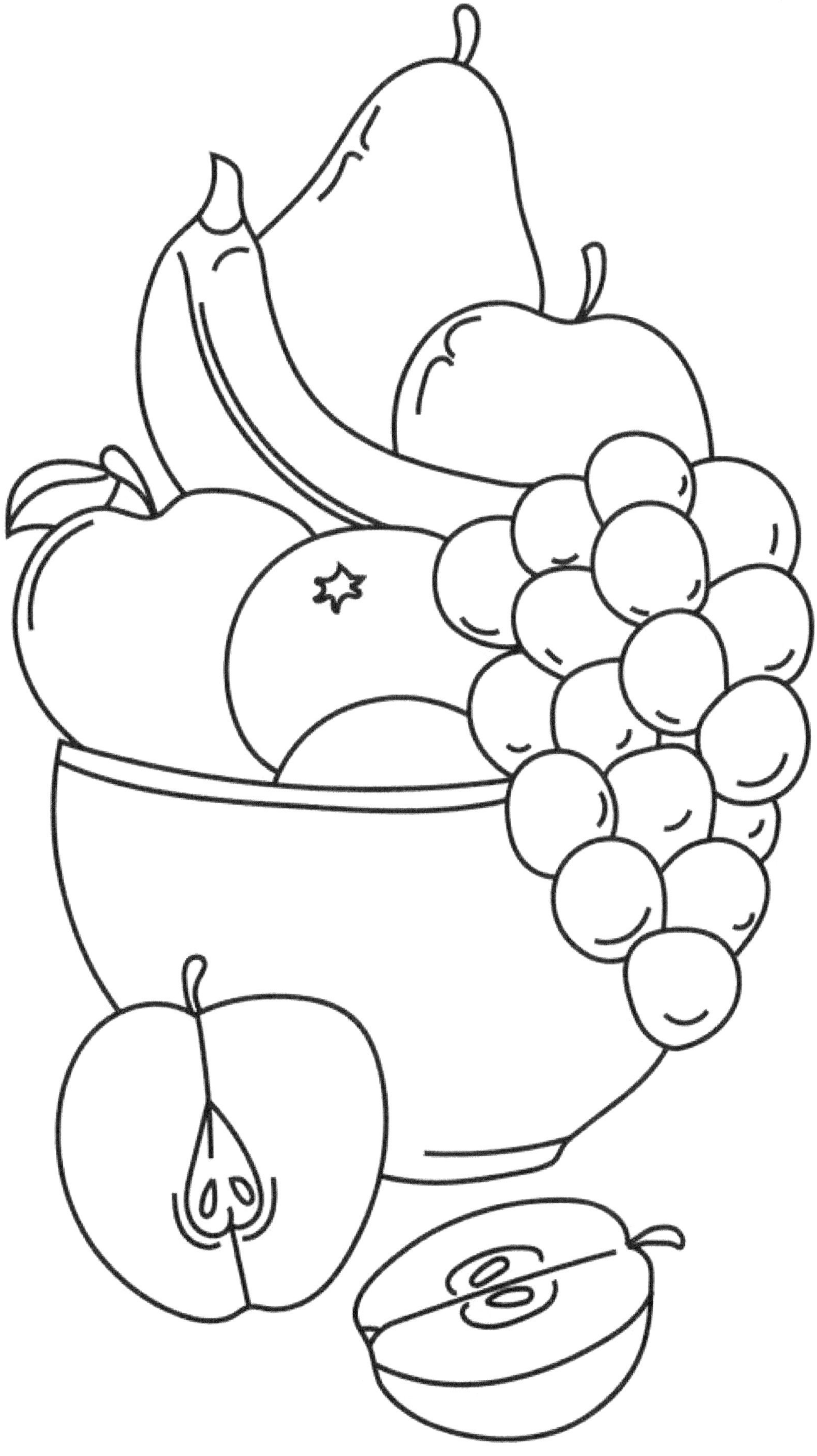

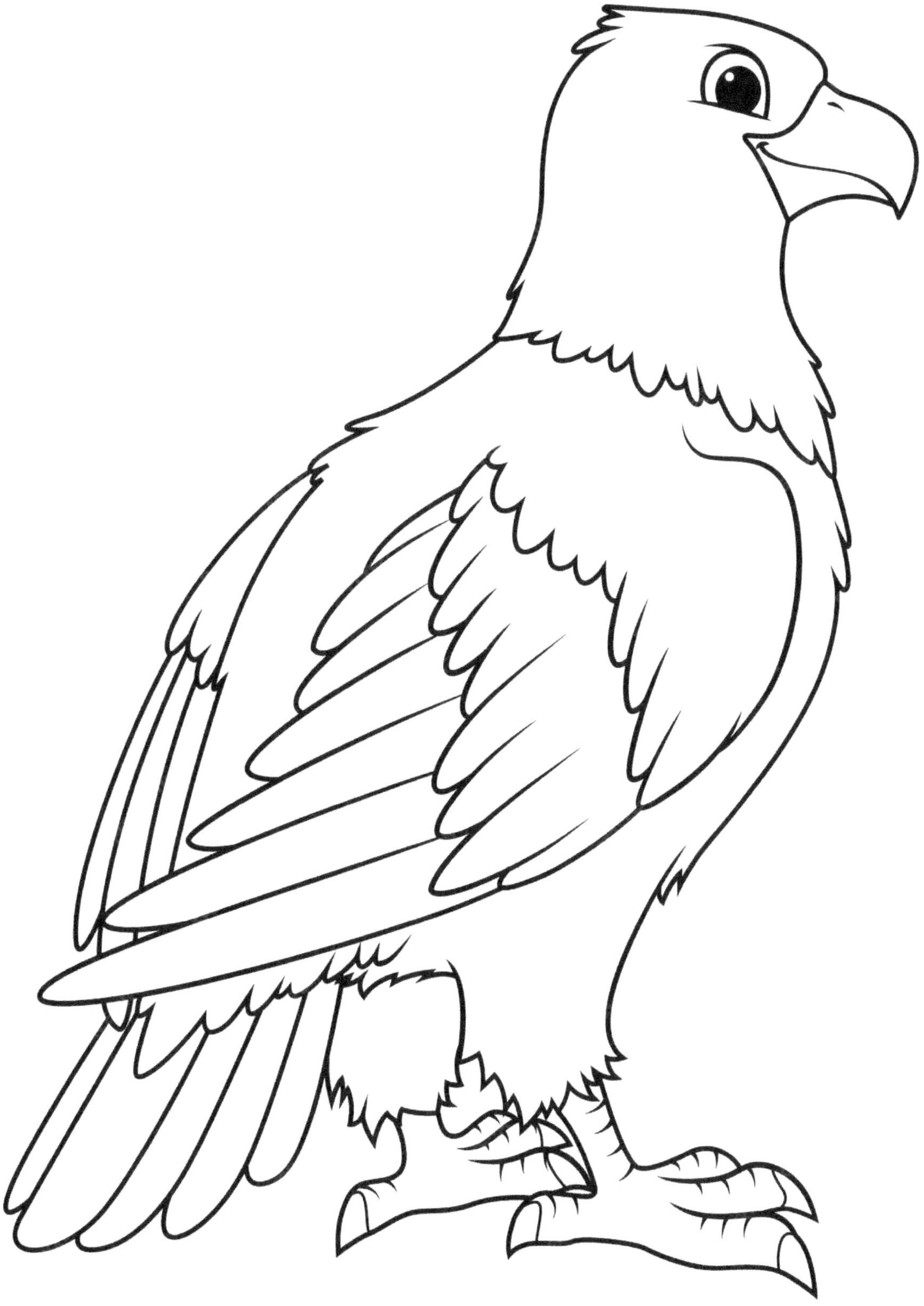

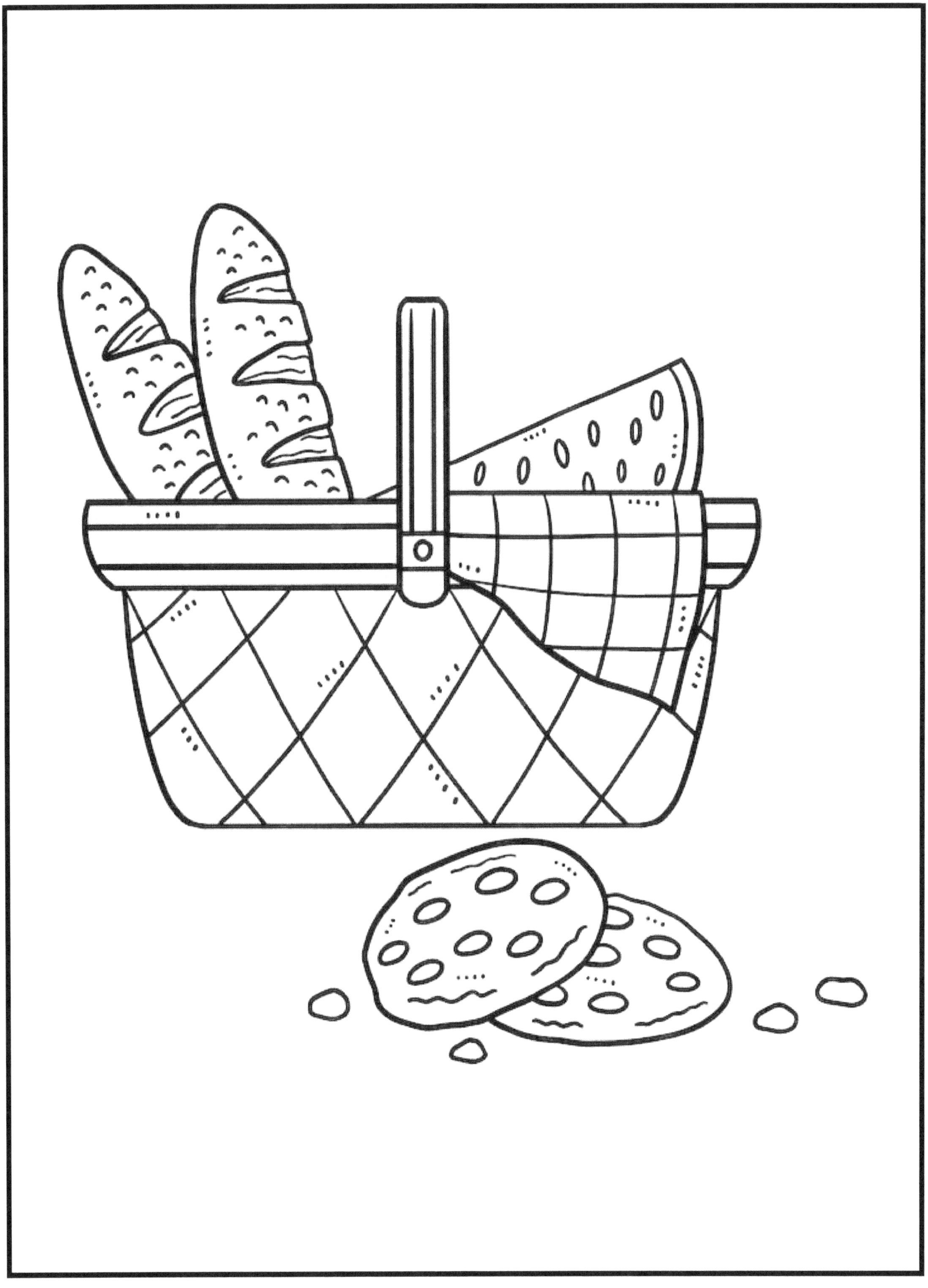

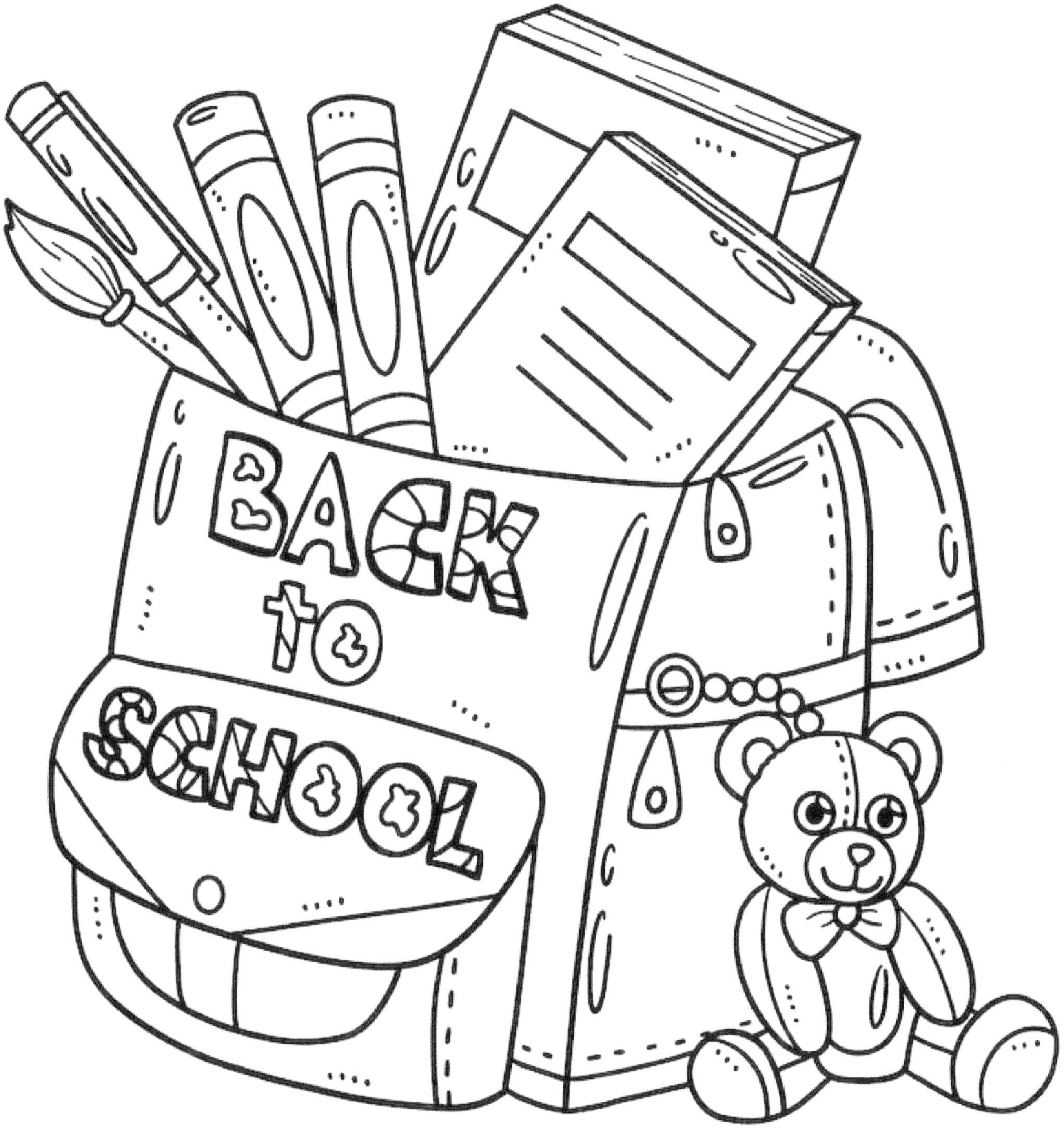
BACK
TO
SCHOOL

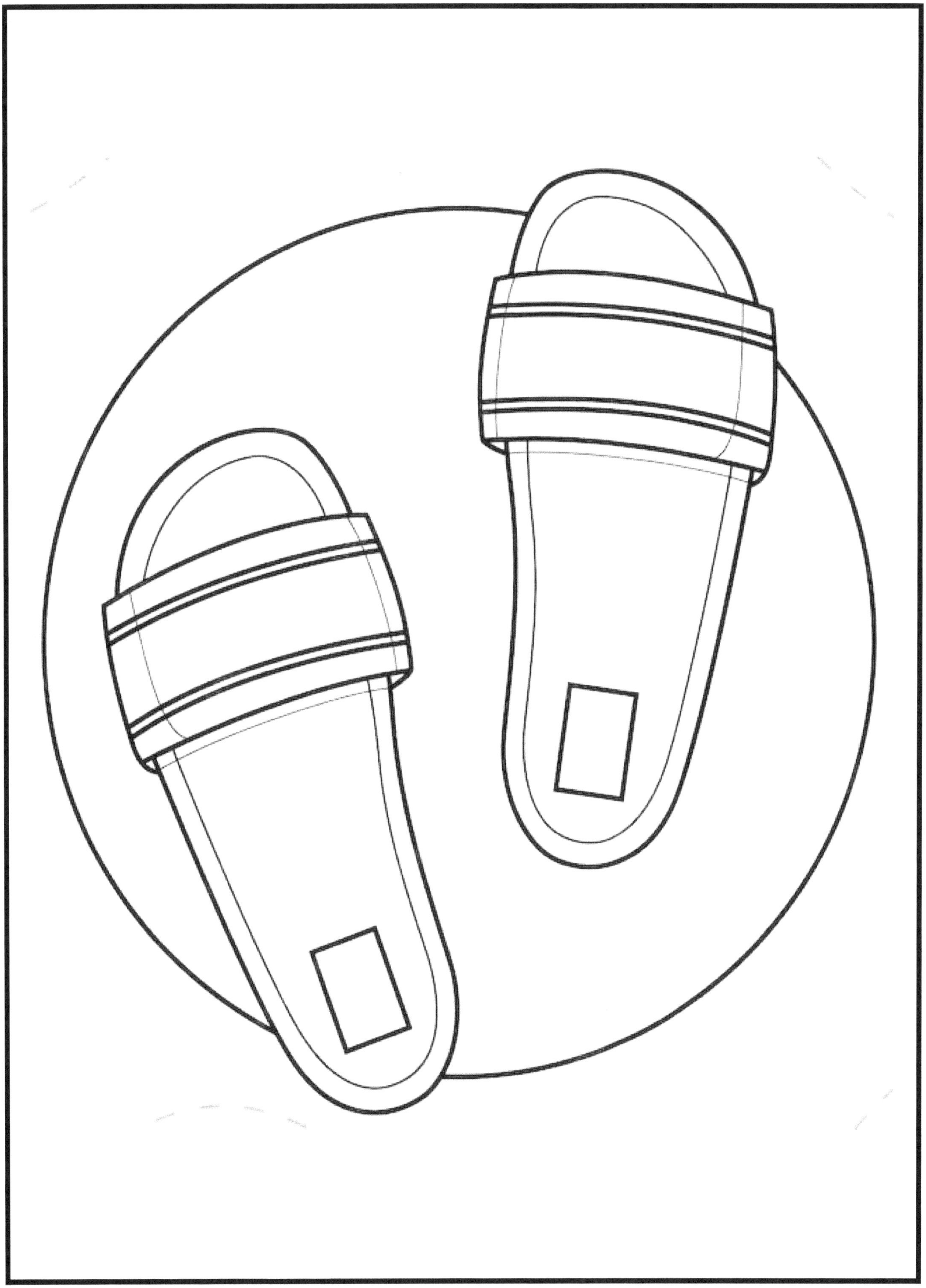

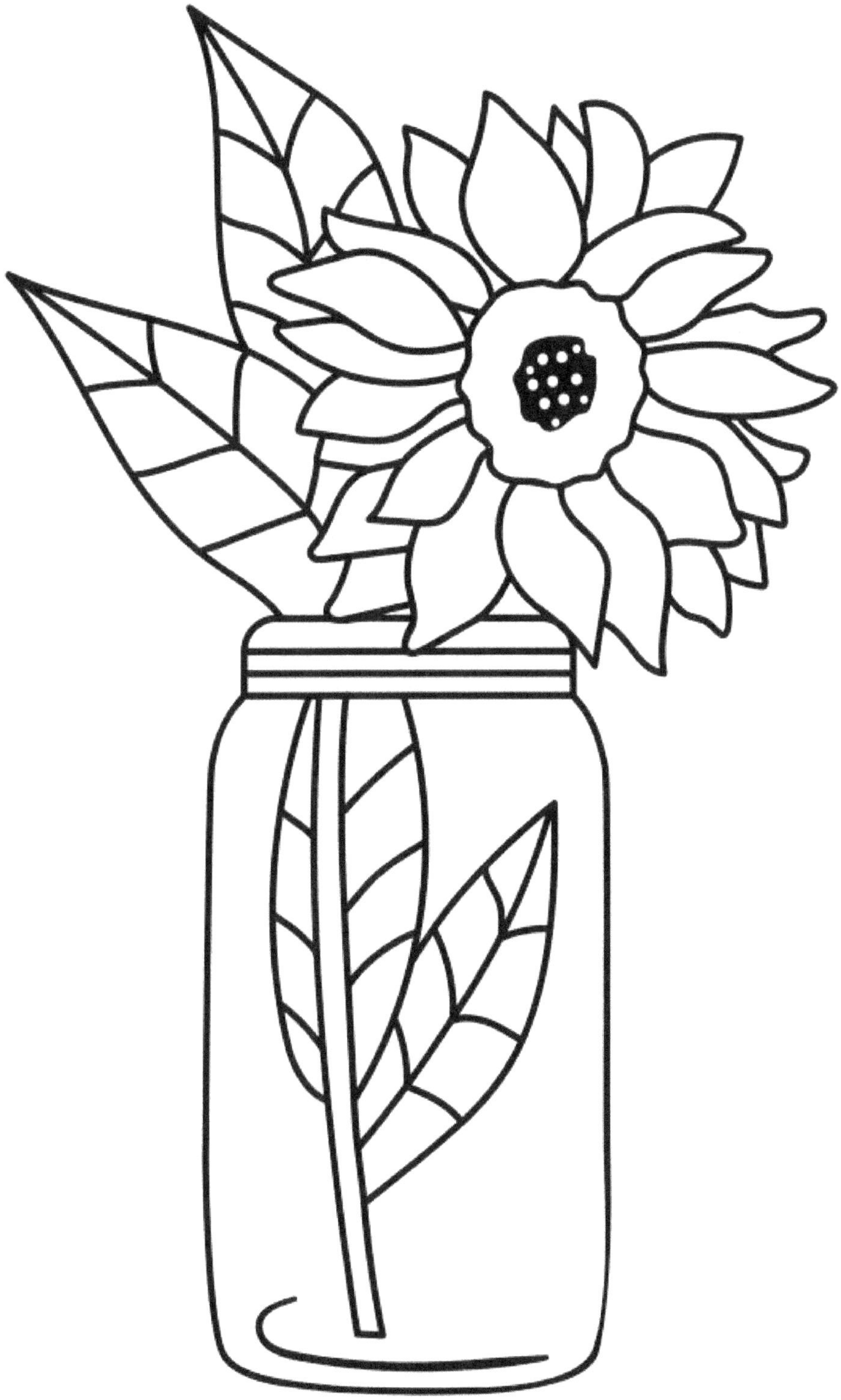

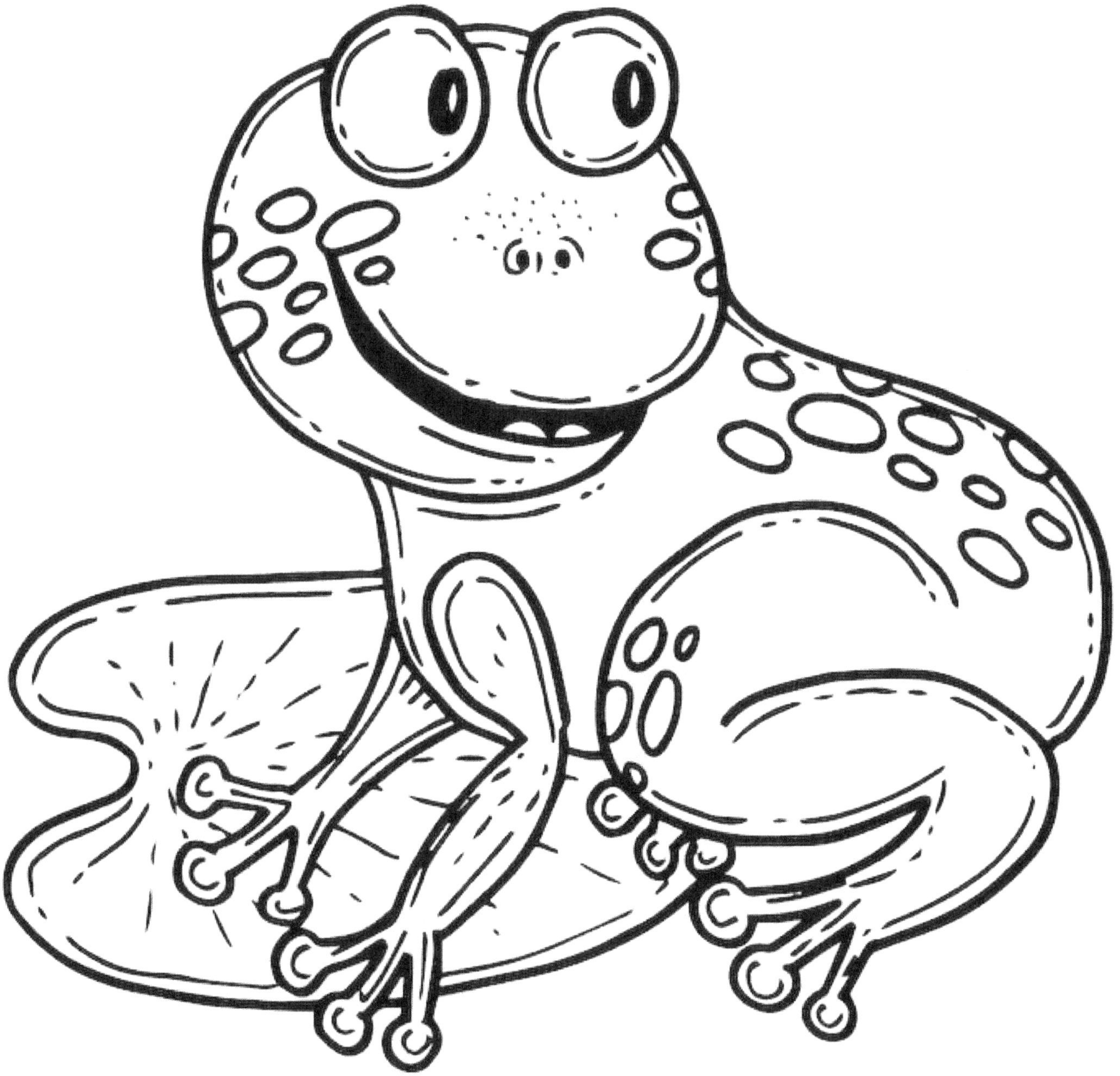

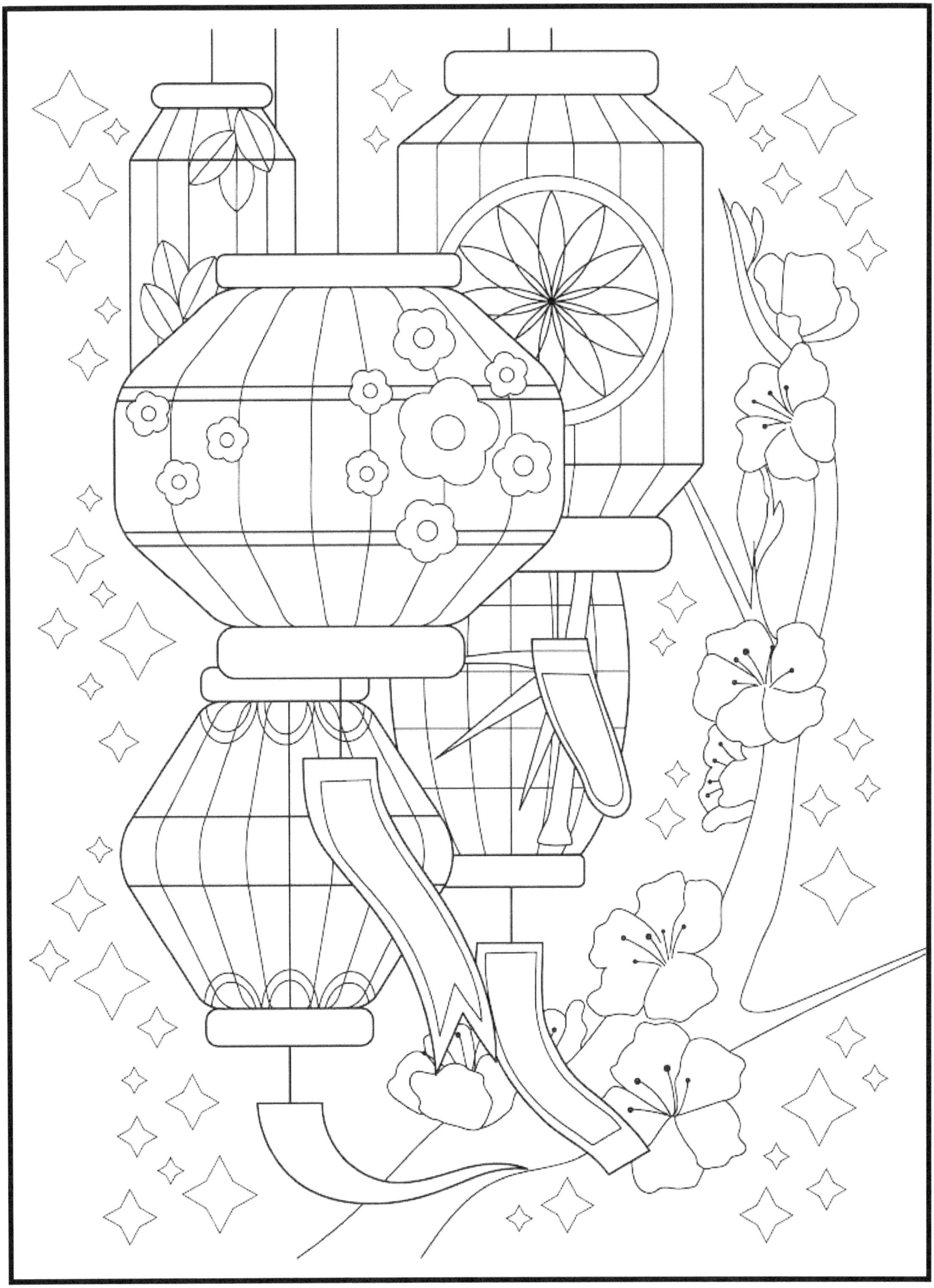

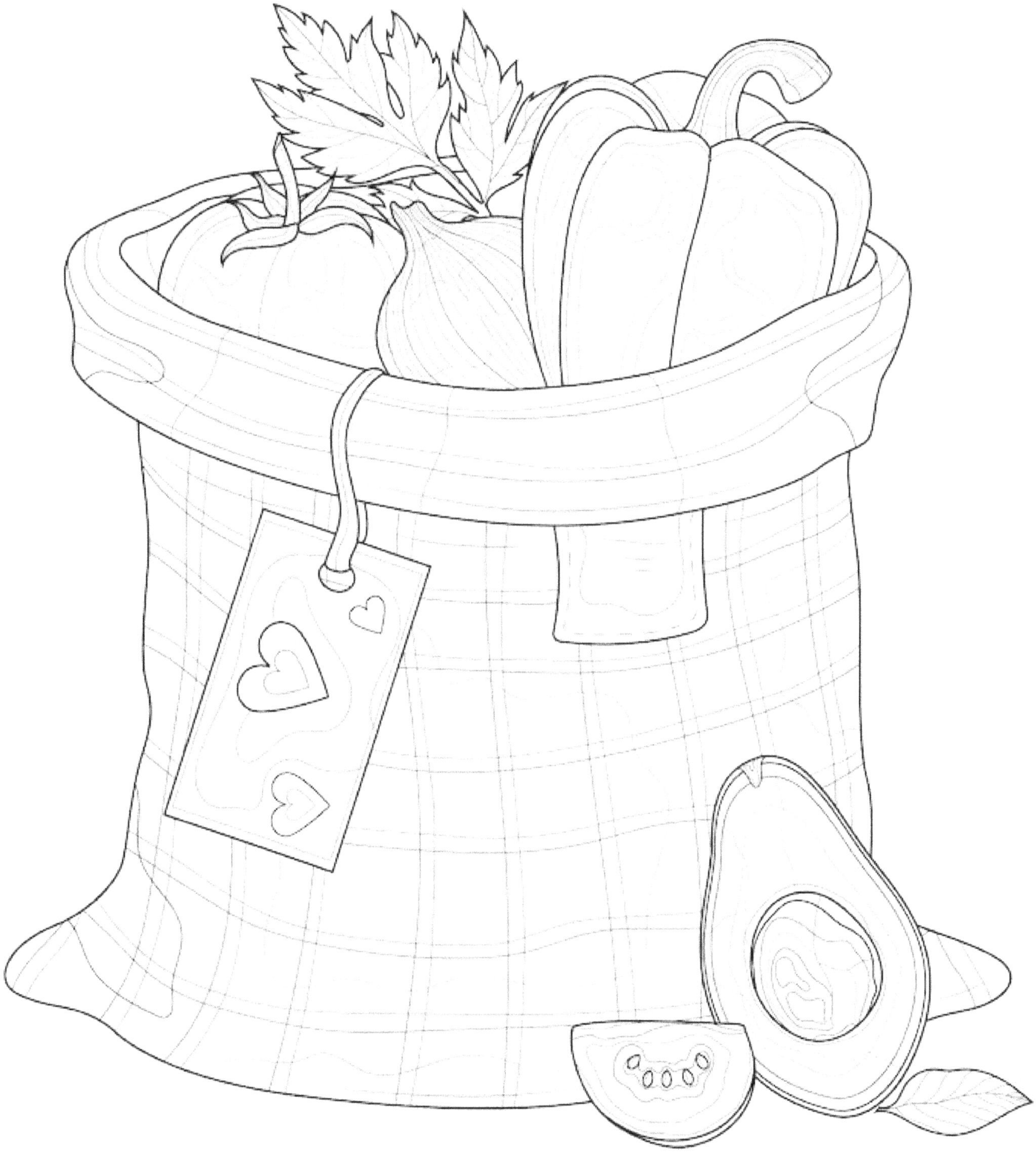

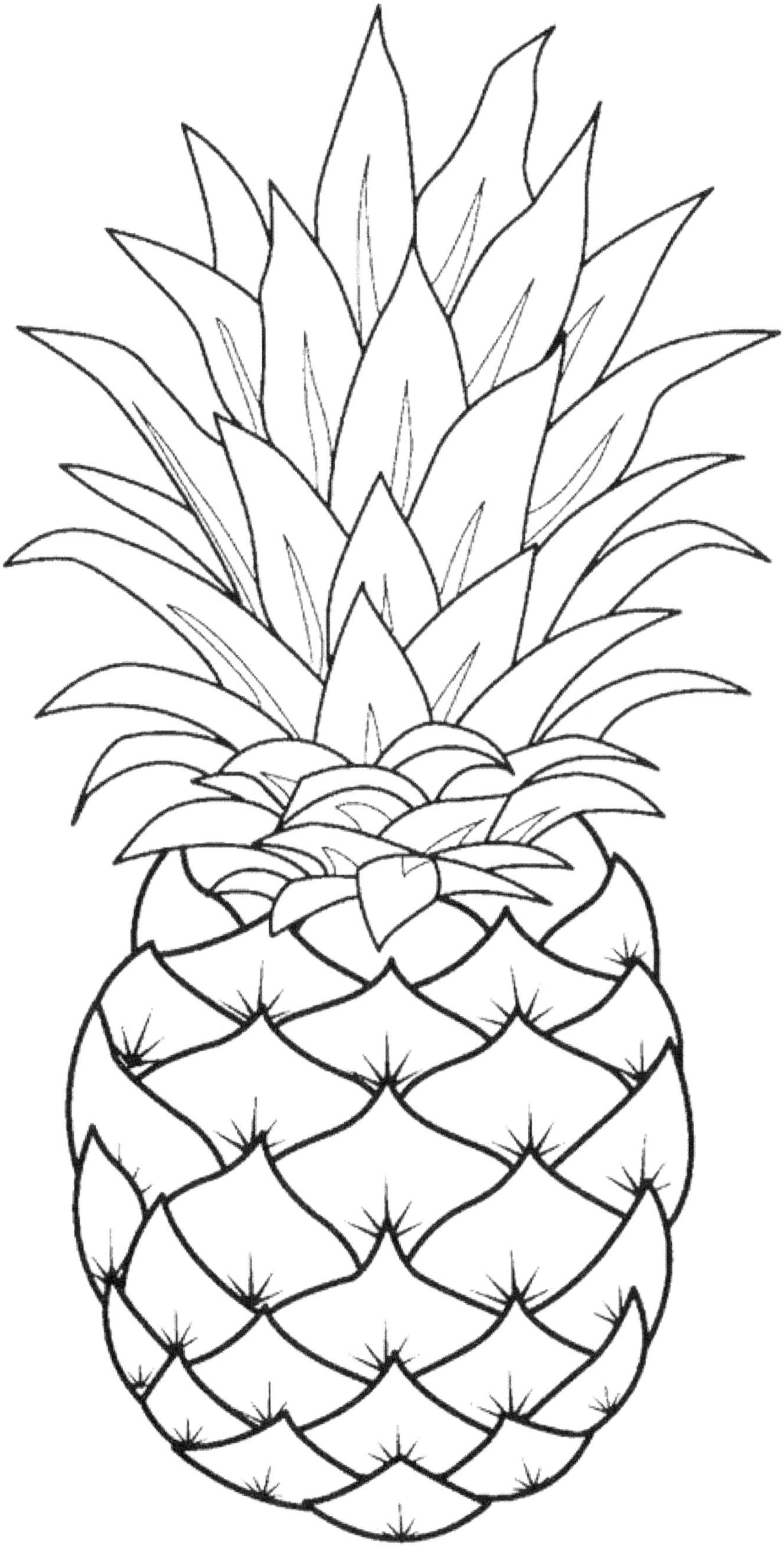

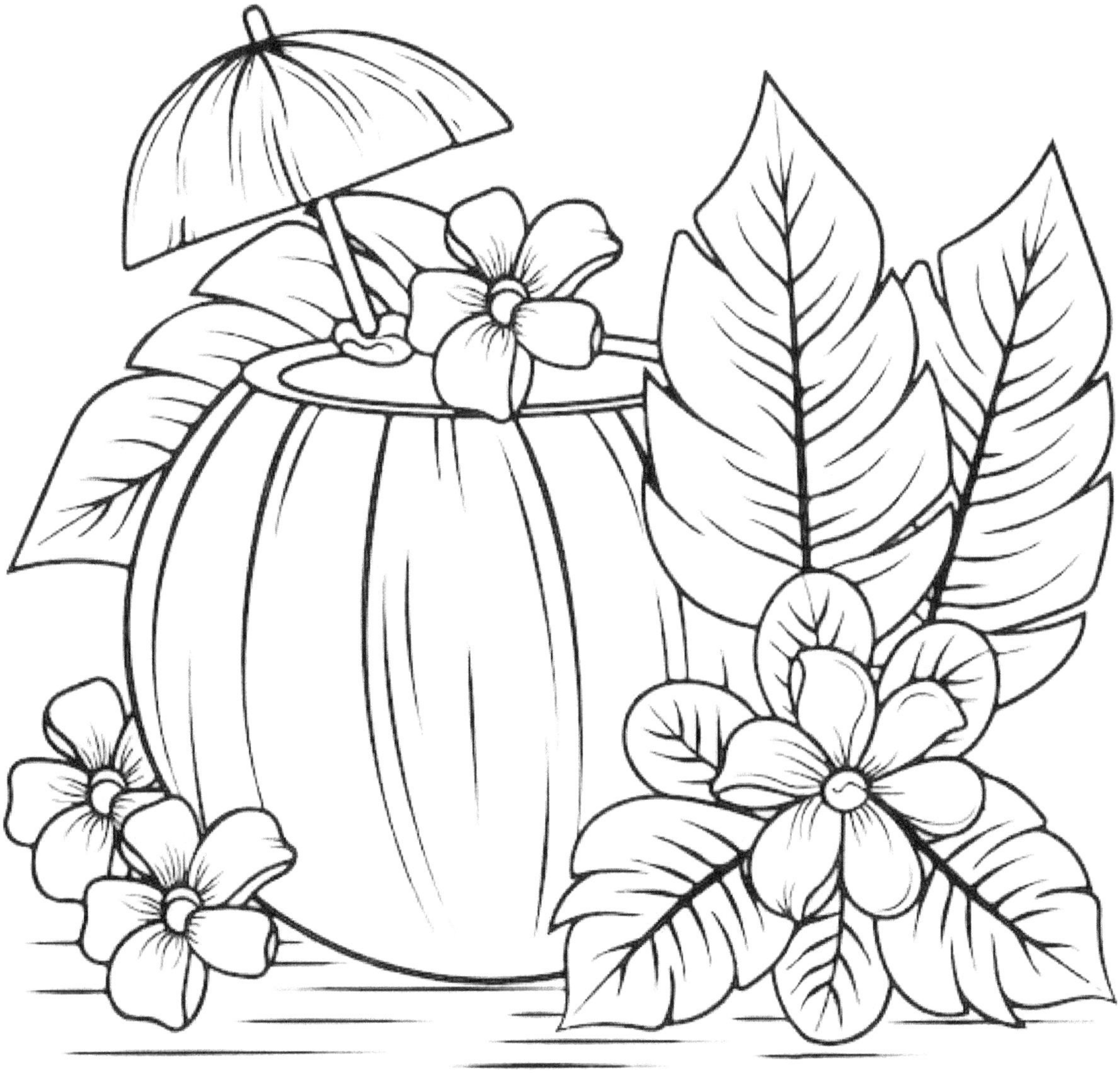

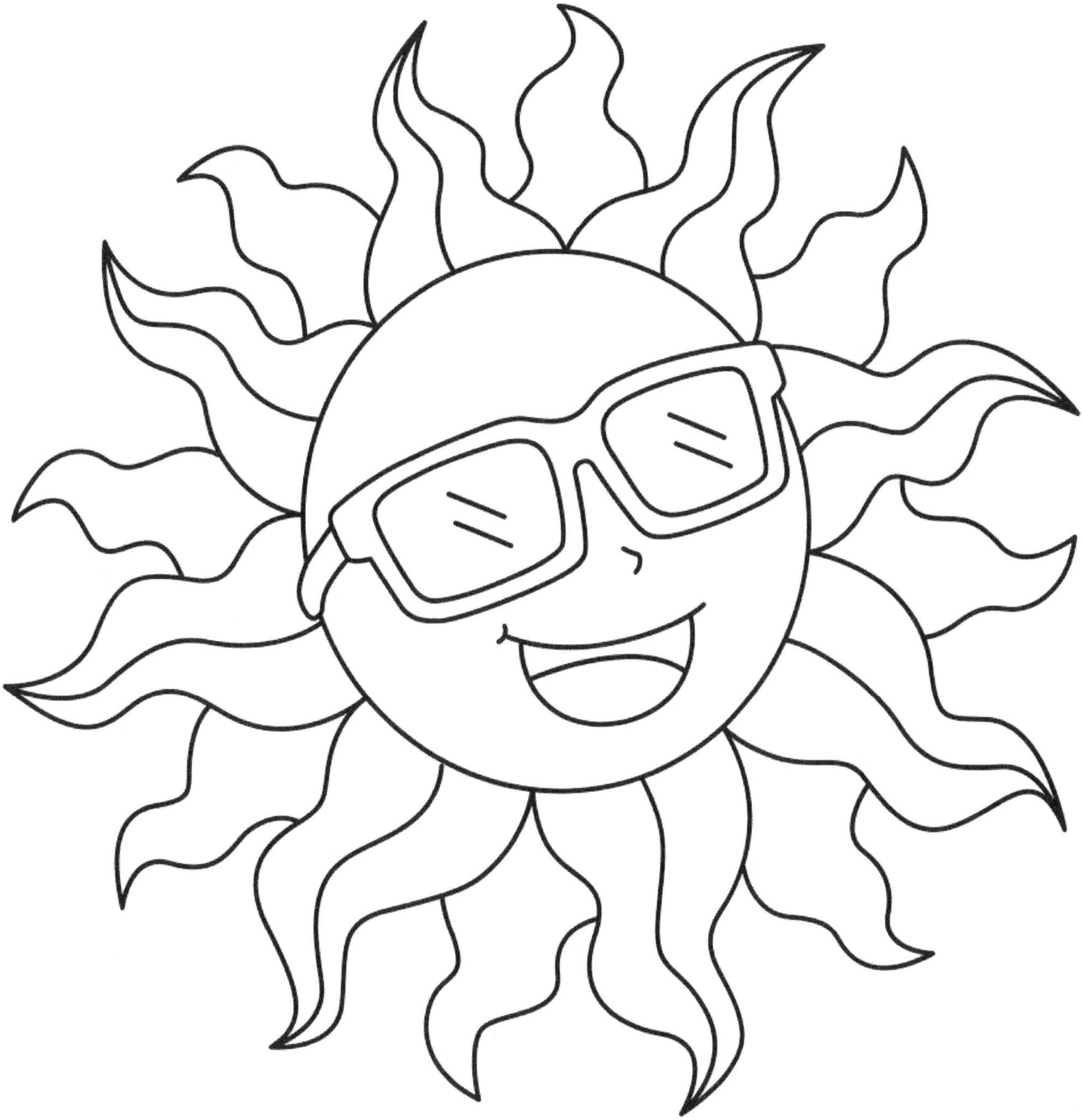

www.ingramcontent.com/pod-product-compliance
Lightning Source LLC
Chambersburg PA
CBHW062112220526
45471CB00010B/3702
* 9 7 9 8 3 2 3 1 6 9 1 9 1 *